M000250267

THE COMPLETE GUIDE TO MORKIES

David Anderson

Cover photo courtesy of Kim Moore

Copyright © 2018 David Anderson
All rights reserved.

TABLE OF CONTENTS

Introduction 6

CHAPTER ONE

What is a Morkie? 8
Is it a Yorkie or a Maltese? 8
Morkie personality traits 12
Your Morkie's family history 14
Interesting facts about Morkies 16

CHAPTER TWO

Is a Morkie puppy for you? 18
The ideal family for a Morkie 19
Pros and cons of having a Morkie 22
Adopting an older Morkie 24
Morkies and other dogs 25
Ideal habitat for a Morkie 25
Where should you buy your Morkie? 28

CHAPTER THREE

How to prepare your house for your Morkie puppy 30
How to puppy-proof your home 30
House rules and routines 34
Supplies to have on hand 38
Service providers 41
The journey home 42

CHAPTER FOUR

Potty training 48
Be prepared from day one 48
How to potty train your Morkie 53
To crate train or den train 58
Clean-up advice 64

Dos and Don'ts in potty training **66**
Litter training your Morkie **70**
How to potty train an older Morkie **73**

CHAPTER FIVE
Obedience training **76**
How to train **76**
Teach with love, not fear **80**
Say no to barking **82**
Patience is a virtue **86**
Training and rewards **87**
Leash training **89**

CHAPTER SIX
How to care for your Morkie **92**
Grooming basics **92**
Anal glands **108**
Tearstains **110**
Tools needed for grooming **113**
Going to the groomer **114**
Exercise **119**

CHAPTER SEVEN
Your Morkie's dietary needs **122**
Daily nutritional needs **122**
How much is too much? **124**
Commercial dog food vs. homemade dog food **125**
How to choose a wholesome commercial dog food **129**
How to make a wholesome homemade dog food **131**
Foods to avoid **134**
Simple recipes for your Morkie **136**

CHAPTER EIGHT
Morkies and their health **146**
Vaccinations **146**
Neutering and spaying **147**
Future health concerns and how to prevent them **150**
How to choose a good veterinarian **152**

CHAPTER NINE

Common behavior issues **154**
How to stop your Morkie from having bad habits **155**
Socializing with other dogs **163**
Socializing with all types of people **165**
Learning to accept the postman **166**

Conclusion **170**

*Photo Courtesy of
Ray Williams*

Introduction

Have you ever closely observed a snowflake, perhaps comparing it to other snowflakes? If you have, you surely noticed that each snowflake is different. Scientists say that if you studied every snowflake ever made; you would not find an exact duplicate, each one being very unique.

But what do snowflakes have to do with your Morkie puppy?

Just as no two snowflakes are alike, all dogs and especially Morkies have their own unique traits.

Morkies are a crossbreed of the Maltese and the Yorkshire terrier, bringing out the best of each breed. This crossbreed might possibly be the perfect dog. It is the ideal companion dog that loves to cuddle and has the exact dose of spunk to keep you active.

The purpose of this book is to define the common characteristics of Morkies in general. You will discover your Morkie's outstanding qualities and traits and learn how to give it the best life ever.

This book will give you a thorough background of your Morkie's family history, which will make its personality become even more endearing.

It will also teach you how to work with your Morkie's moldable personality and teach it to be a delightful little angel. You will learn how to create the perfect environment to teach your Morkie and how to avoid creating bad habits that will come back to haunt you later on in life.

Common behavior issues are discussed in this book, providing troubleshooting and strategies on how to fix bad habits or behavior. There is a whole chapter dedicated to one of the most challenging aspects of obedience training, potty training.

You will also learn the essentials of proper nutrition for your Morkie and how to choose the best dog food for your loveable puppy. A Morkie can be one of life's most rewarding experiences. They can relieve our stress, improve our health and remind us that true love does exist. You will find raising your Morkie to be one of the richest and most satisfying experiences of your life.

This book will become your go-to guide throughout your Morkie's life, as it has helpful hints and reminders that will prove to be practical far into your Morkie's adulthood.

Can you raise the perfect dog?

Absolutely!

Your little bundle of joy will be the proof that a perfect dog does exist. It just requires some patience and love on your part to apply the helpful suggestions found in this book.

CHAPTER ONE
What is a Morkie?

The Morkie takes the gentleness of the Maltese, combines it with the sassiness of the Yorkie, and leaves you with a playful, loving, lap dog, with amazing color variations!"

Karen Dawn Thomas
www.angellinekennels.com

Morkies are absolutely adorable. A common reaction when seeing a Morkie is a squeal of delight. This crossbreed is very tiny with long hair that makes it resemble a Ewok from Star Wars, and who doesn't love Ewoks?

Morkies are considered to be one of the world's cutest crossbreeds. From the very first day you bring your Morkie home, it will have stolen your heart, with its big, baby doll eyes and upbeat personality.

Morkies are a perfect choice for all types of dog lovers. If you just don't have the space for a larger dog and you love being able to cuddle with your dog on your lap, Morkies are the ideal lap dog. They love daily long cuddles.

In this book, we will discuss some basic information about your Morkie and how you can give it the best life ever. But what exactly is a Morkie?

Is it a Yorkie or a Maltese?

Morkies are considered to be a crossbreed, so they aren't classified as a purebred. Crossbreeds are the result of two different breeds of dog bred together. Normally, breeders will breed two popular but different types of purebreds together, such in the case of your Morkie. Morkies are a crossbreed of a purebred Yorkshire terrier and a Maltese, bringing out the best in each breed.

Crossbreeding a Yorkshire terrier and a Maltese produces a happy, intelligent and friendly dog. Morkies are considered to be one of the world's most adorable crossbreeds. Their size makes them ideal for being a lapdog and they have been called the eternal puppy.

How long will my Morkie live?

When it comes to longevity, your Morkie has a lot going for it.

Yorkshire terriers live fourteen to sixteen years. They are sturdy little terriers with a truckload of energy and strength for their tiny size. They were originally bred to hunt rats in northern England and Scotland.

The Maltese is one of the world's most elegant breeds and has a life span of twelve to fourteen years. It is one of the most ancient breeds on the planet, dating back more than twenty-eight centuries.

Morkies will typically live for about fourteen years. But the age your Morkie will live to will depend on its health. How can you ensure your Morkie lives as long as possible?

- Keep it at a healthy weight.
- Have it annually checked by a certified veterinarian.
- Give it a wholesome healthy diet.

Morkie fur colors

If you have had your Morkie for a couple weeks already, you might have already noticed a drastic change in its hair color since the day you brought it home. Why is that?

Morkies are constantly changing their hair color because of the inherited genes from one of their parents, the Yorkshire terrier. Morkie puppies can come in a wide variety of colors such as white, brown, tan and black. It is normal for an all-black Morkie puppy's fur to begin to lighten as it ages.

The reason for this is inherited genes from the Yorkshire terrier, as most Yorkies turn into a shiny, golden, silvery grey or tan color once they reach maturity. Yorkies tend to have more dominant genes than the Maltese. Morkies tend to look more like their Yorkie parent, but if you find an all-white Morkie, the dominant gene will be the Maltese.

No matter what type or color of fur your Morkie has inherited, it will still need to be regularly groomed, brushed, bathed and trimmed, to keep it looking its best.

Both Maltese and Morkies have long thin hair, if not trimmed regularly. Yorkies have a silkier coat that doesn't tend to mat as easily as Maltese, which have very thin cotton-like hair.

Here is a brief description of your Morkie's parents' colors and how they might affect your Morkie.

Yorkshire Terriers: Yorkies are never one solid color, but typically have a blue/gold coloring. Yorkies can have only four different colors: tan, gold, black and blue. Normally, Yorkie puppies are black and tan and the coloring changes in their adult years to a bluish-grey and golden tone.

If the breeder's Yorkshire terrier does not have the bluish and golden hair color, then it is not a purebred Yorkie and you had best continue looking for another breeder. There is no such thing as a solid colored Yorkshire terrier.

Yorkshire terriers change from black to tan in the period of their first two or maybe three years. The bluish fur is not really blue but more like a diluted blackish-grey color.

Maltese: Many believe that Maltese can only be found in one solid color, stark snow white. But there are other colors. Pure snow white is the preferred color, but the other two colors Maltese can have are a very light beige color or a soft yellow tone called lemon.

To be classified purebred, a Maltese needs to be pure white on its body and only have light tan or lemon coloring on its ears or around its face. If it has coloring on its back or elsewhere it might have purebred Maltese parents, but somewhere in their lineage they were bred with another breed.

Morkies: Considering your Morkie's parents, it is easy to understand why there is no defined coat color, as it is a crossbreed with an all-white (or mostly white) Maltese and a golden-bluish Yorkie. Colors can range from a solid white to black and tan and every combination and color between those colors.

You can expect your Morkie to change as it gets older, becoming a more diluted tone of this puppy hair. The hardest part will be choosing the cutest Morkie to bring home with you.

Type of fur

Morkies are low-shedding dogs, but there is no such thing as a non-shedding dog unless it is completely bald. All dogs shed just like humans. Shedding is part of our natural hair growth, as hair starts from a follicle, which allows it to grow, and then when it dies is replaced with another follicle. When the follicle dies, it causes the hair to drop or shed.

Each breed of dog has a different time for growing and shedding their fur, some more often than others. The Yorkie and Maltese shed their hair rarely, as they are inside pets and have fine hair instead of fur. Because of this, they are sometimes referred to as hypoallergenic dogs.

Morkies are allergy-friendly if someone is allergic to dog fur, since they have hair and not fur. Morkies can still trigger allergies if someone is allergic to dog dander, saliva, or even urine. So saying that Morkies are hypoallergenic is a myth as no dog is 100 percent hypoallergenic.

Morkies are voted one of the lowest shedding dogs in the world, as they have a single coat of hair.

Facts sheet about Morkie Dogs	
Pronunciation	Mork-ee
Common nicknames	Yorktese
Breed history	Cross between a purebred Yorkshire terrier and a purebred Maltese
Average weight	4 to 8 lbs.
Average height	6 to 8 inches
Life expectancy	10-13 years
Maturity	1 year old considered an adult
Average litter size	2 to 4 puppies
Shedding	Very light shedders
Purpose	Companion, lap dogs
Temperament	Affectionate, playful and stubborn
Best suited for	Families with older children, seniors, singles, apartment dwellers and houses with or without yards

Morkie personality traits

All living creatures inherit genes from their parents, which helps to define their personality traits. Nature comes into play when helping mold our personalities. This is especially true with humans and domesticated pets, but how our personality is nurtured will affect the final outcome.

Have you ever heard the expression "like father, like son"? It means that the son's behavior, conduct and features resemble that of his father, the reason being that the father's genes have been passed on to his child, making his son a smaller version of himself.

With dogs, the same thing happens. They inherit certain personality traits from their parents such as appearance, behavior and even health issues. For this reason, before we can understand the personality traits of a Morkie puppy, we need to know about the pros and cons of the parents, the purebred Maltese and Yorkshire terrier.

Maltese

Some of the *pros* with Maltese are that they don't require too much exercise and can be easily entertained with simple games and toys, such as get-the-ball-out-from-under-the-cabinet. They are very playful and are often happy to play alone. The Maltese isn't a heavy shedder even though it has a beautiful coat of hair. They are very easy to train.

A *con* with Maltese puppies is that they are extremely difficult to potty train. Also, because of their size, they are very fragile. Because of this, it is not recommended to have them with families with small children or bigger dogs that might decide the Maltese would make a good afternoon snack. They are also high-maintenance with grooming and suffer from chronic allergies and itchy skin.

Yorkshire terrier

Yorkshire terriers have many *pros*, like being so tiny they are easy to fit into your purse or be carried around. Also, since they are small dogs they don't require too much exercise, making them an ideal pet for people with small apartments and the elderly. Yorkshire terriers don't have a long list of illnesses that will affect them later on in life. Yorkies are very easy to train and are very faithful to their owners.

There are also few *cons* with Yorkshire terriers. They have a little stubborn streak when it comes to potty training, but with consistency and an extra dose of patience, they will learn. Also, because of their size, their bones can break from a fall and they are sensitive to warm or cold temperatures. If you travel often or leave your Yorkie home alone, it is likely to suffer from acute separation anxiety that will be extremely difficult to correct later on. They are also high-maintenance with grooming.

The Yorkshire terrier and the Maltese make the ideal combination for your Morkie's parents, bringing out the best of each breed and producing the world's cutest dog. So what are some of the outstanding personality traits of the Morkie?

Pros:

Playful and social: Morkies thrive on companionship and strive to please their owners. Their only desire is to make you happy and they will have you smiling and laughing within minutes. They are extremely good tempered and get along with other dogs.

Intelligent: Yorkshire terriers are very intelligent and they have passed their intelligence to their offspring, the Morkie. They can easily be taught a number of obedience commands.

Exercise: They don't require too much exercise; two or three short brisk walks around the block or to the park each day are enough to tucker them out. They are happy living in a small apartment, as they don't need too much space to run around.

Photo Courtesy of Margherita Sansone

Cons:

Fragile: Morkies are very fragile, small and delicate. Make sure that if young children are around, they are supervised and they understand that they need to be gentle with your Morkie, as they could easily break its bones.

High-maintenance: Your Morkie has inherited beautiful long hair from both parents, the Yorkie and the Maltese. It will need to be brushed daily and groomed regularly by a professional groomer.

Separation anxiety: If you leave your Morkie home alone often, the chances that your Morkie will suffer from separation anxiety are great. Make sure that you hire a dog sitter if you are going to leave it alone for long periods.

As we can see, the Morkie crossbreed produces a very affectionate and playful puppy. A Morkie's energy level will depend on which breed's genes dominate. If the Yorkie's energy level dominates, it will be a more hyperactive pup; but if the Maltese breed's genes dominate, it will be a more laid-back pup.

Your Morkie's family history

Morkies' history began in the Unites States with breeders in search of the perfect lap dog. Some historians state that the first Morkie was bred in Quebec, Canada in the 1990's. Needless to say, wherever the first Morkie was bred, perfection was achieved and it's called a Morkie.

Morkies are considered to be a crossbreed and are not recognized by the American Kennel Club as a purebred. Dogs that have been cross-bred are often called "designer dogs".

A crossbreed dog is the result of breeding one purebred dog to a different purebred dog. Morkies are a crossbreed of the Yorkshire terrier and the Maltese.

Dogs that have been crossbred have become more popular in the past fifteen years or so, due to the belief that crossbreeds will be healthier and stronger than their purebred parents. When the lineage for cross-breeding is correctly chosen, the outcome can be a puppy worth more than its purebred parents.

Now that you understand crossbreeding, here is quick overview of your Morkie's family history.

Maltese:

The Maltese dog's history goes back to about 500 B.C. This breed was recorded on a Greek Amphora. The breed's name and origins are believed to have come from the Mediterranean Island of Malta. History suggests that it was bred to help control rodents, but soon became popular among the noble women. Maltese dogs have been highly esteemed as a ladies' dog throughout the ages and up until our day.

Maltese

Yorkshire terrier:

Yorkies are a newer breed; no more than a hundred years ago they were bred for the purpose of catching rats in mills in England. They are also often used for hunting as they can burrow underground to catch badgers and foxes. Yorkies have been voted year after year one of American Kennel Club's "most popular" dog breeds. Most Yorkie owners will agree with that statement, as they are beautiful, fearless, feisty and extremely loyal.

As we can see, Morkies have a rich history. But your Morkie will instantly become part of your own family history from the minute you bring it home.

Yorkshire Terrier

Morkies are happy-go-lucky dogs that love to play hard and then cuddle up on the couch.

Interesting facts about Morkies

When your Morkie is born, it only weighs about four to five ounces and is smaller than a tennis ball. Even a full-grown Morkie will only weigh an average of 4 to 7 pounds, making it the perfect lap dog. It will even fit perfectly into your purse for walking around town.

Since your Morkie is so tiny at birth (and even when fully grown!) it will need to be handled with special care and love. Morkies can easily fall and break a bone; always avoid playing roughly with your Morkie.

Normally a litter of Morkies is small, no more than two to four puppies per litter, since the Maltese and Yorkshire terrier are very small in size. Because litters are so small, it can be hard to find a Morkie from a reputable breeder. You most likely will have order yours far in advance.

Morkies thrive on human companionship and quickly become attached to their new families. Because of this tight bond, training will be needed to avoid separation anxiety later on. Your Morkie's love for its family can create problems when it is left home alone.

Morkies are best suited for families without small children, as children tend to play roughly with dogs. Morkies are happy in most environments, from a house in the suburbs with a big yard to a miniscule city apartment.

Morkie enthusiasts are developing their own purebred dogs that will be accepted and recognized by registries such as the American Kennel Club and the Canadian Kennel Club, but this may take decades to do.

Unlike other crossbreds, it is possible to breed two Morkies and have favorable results. The original cross is considered to be a true cross, as it is between two different purebred dogs. In some cases, breeding two Morkies together can result in a more reliable temperament and appearance.

Your Morkie might be tiny, but it has a ferocious appetite and loves to eat. Morkies tend to have dental issues later on in life. If you don't plan on cleaning its teeth once or twice a week, it is preferable that you feed it high-quality dry dog food. Dry dog food helps to prevent the buildup of plaque which results in cavities and other dental concerns.

Since Morkies live to eat, you will need to keep a close eye on your dog's weight. Because of their size, Morkies are prone to becoming overweight, even obese. Make sure your Morkie gets enough exercise and isn't receiving too many snacks. If your dog is overweight, it can lead to future health problems that can be very painful and costly.

Morkies are easy to train but they have a stubborn streak at times. You will need to be patient and gentle with your training, as harsh training methods will cause your Morkie to shut down and stop learning. All training sessions should be happy and positive with lots of praise and yummy treats, which will turn your stubborn Morkie into a wonderful student.

CHAPTER TWO
Is a Morkie puppy for you?

"Do lots of research on breeders and ONLY buy from a reputable breeder that has healthy friendly dogs. Find a breeder that will stand behind their dogs and help you if you have questions or issues in the future. "

Pam Peterson
www.royalkennels.com

A dog is a man's best friend.
If you have ever had a dog before, you are surely in agreement with those words. Having a dog can be one of life's most rewarding experiences. Dogs give us their companionship and unconditional love without asking for anything in return except love.

Studies have proven that having a dog can bring many health benefits, such as lowering blood pressure, warding off depression and reducing stress.

Another advantage to having a dog is that it is a surefire way to get daily exercise. Your Morkie will need at least two thirty-minute walks daily, which means you will be getting exercise too. A dog is a great motivational tool to get you off your couch and out for a nice brisk walk.

Dogs have the capability to make the world's grumpiest person break down and smile in a matter of seconds. They make us feel loved and cared for and are always ready to happily greet us when we walk through the front door.

Choosing which type of puppy to bring home and become your new best friend can be a very daunting experience. With so many different types of dogs, how can you know if a Morkie puppy is right for you?

The ideal family for a Morkie

Living environment

Morkies are very sensitive to climate changes, cold and hot weather. The reality is that your Morkie cannot live outside. It cannot survive outside for long periods. Morkies are meant to live inside with you and cuddle on your lap, as they are smaller than most cats. They require a warm, cozy living environment.

Also, because of their size, they have absolutely no means to defend themselves against larger dogs or birds of prey. Leaving your Morkie outside for long periods of a time, can also cause your Morkie to become overly stressed out and cause it to suffer from separation anxiety.

Morkies need to spend the majority of their time inside of your house where they feel safe and sound and near to you. Morkies can't tolerate cold and hot weather. In the cold winter months, you might need to get a little sweater for your Morkie to prevent it from getting sick when going outside for walks and potty breaks.

✔ *If you plan on having your Morkie pup live indoors with you and be part of your family, then a Morkie is the dog for you.*

Photo Courtesy of
Kellie Whitton

Also, Morkies make ideal pets for those who live in an apartment building or have a very small yard. They don't need too much space to burn off their excess energy. The best way to burn off your Morkie's energy is to take it for short walks around the block.

✔ *If you live in an apartment building or have a small yard, then a Morkie is the dog for you.*

Maintenance

Your Morkie has inherited its lovely coat from its parents, the Maltese and the Yorkshire terrier. But sadly those beautiful locks can easily become matted and knotted, which causes your pet to be uncomfortable, to have itchy skin and shed a lot. How can you avoid this?

Daily brushing is the key to preventing the coat from forming unsightly knots and hairballs. Yorkshire terriers, Maltese and Morkies are low shedders, which makes them ideal for allergy sufferers.

Morkies are considered to be high-maintenance because you have to brush them daily, but really compared to the time you would spend vacuuming your house and furniture from the all the hair that your dog sheds, spending less than five minutes a day grooming your dog is a breeze.

✔ *If you have five minutes a day to pamper your dog by brushing it and you dislike finding dog hair all over your house, then a Morkies is the dog for you.*

As with most indoor dogs, it is highly recommended to bathe your pup every three weeks or so to prevent itchy, dry skin.

New dog owners

For new dog owners, it can feel very intimidating to bring home a little puppy, especially when it has to do with potty training. Morkies are very intelligent and are fast learners.

They respond well to firm but loving discipline. Training doesn't require too much time or effort. You need to show your little Morkie that you are the "head of the pack" or the boss.

Normally, a firm "NO" is all it takes to get the message through. Morkie pups are eager to please their owners and are not as stubborn as other small dogs.

✔ *If this is the first puppy in your life and you are nervous about training, then a Morkie is for you, as it is an easy dog to train.*

Be cautious about spoiling it when it is a puppy, as it will turn into a disobedient 'bratty' dog when it gets older.

Small children and large dogs

If you have small children or little grandchildren that often come over to your house, it is not recommended to have a Morkie.

No matter how many times you tell little ones not to handle or pick up your little puppy, they will not be able to resist the temptation. Little ones can accidently drop or squeeze your little puppy too hard and fracture a bone or cause other damage.

✗ *If you have little children over to your house often, it isn't recommended to get a Morkie.*

If you have larger dogs, they may have the tendency to play roughly with smaller dogs. Chances are your little Morkie will suffer dire consequences.

If you do have older dogs, they might be suitable companions for a Morkie because they aren't as rambunctious as younger dogs.

✗ *If you have larger dogs that are hyperactive, it isn't recommended to get a Morkie.*

It might be considered if your large hyperactive dogs are outside dogs and the time spent with your baby Morkie outside will be supervised. This way, there won't be any sad accidents from your pups playing too roughly.

Separation Anxiety

Morkies bond very quickly and closely to their owners and when their people are not around; they can quickly become concerned and worried and even go into panic mode. This is separation anxiety.

Anxiety can turn the most laid-back dog into a destructive monster, chewing on anything that is in front of it, barking, whining and creating chaos throughout the house.

Morkies thrive in environments where there is someone home during the day or if you can take your dog to work with you. Morkies are extremely social and just love being around people.

✗ *If you are planning on leaving your Morkie alone frequently, it isn't recommended to get a Morkie.*

Your Morkie will want to be part of the action with you and other family members. If it is confined and unable to reach you, it may have the tendency to go into panic mode, or at best, whine and bark constantly.

If you decide to have a Morkie, you must realize that it will have free run of your apartment and will not be happy living in the laundry room.

Pros and cons of having a Morkie

Everything in life has pros and cons. With many things, the cons unfortunately seem to outweigh the pros. But this isn't the case with a Morkie.

Pros

- Morkies are extremely intelligent, so they are very easy to house-train. They also respond well to litter box training for those that live in high-rise apartment buildings.
- They are wonderful dogs for first time puppy owners because of their desire to want to please their owners. They are quick learners and respond to love.
- Morkies are ideal for living in small spaces such as apartments, as their exercise needs are easily satisfied with frequent walks around the block. Having a dog is also a great motivational tool to help you start walking more and get more exercise, which benefits your health.
- Morkies don't shed, so you will have no need to be constantly cleaning up your house to remove the dog hair. Also, your clothes won't be covered with dog hair from every time you decide to pick up your adorable little puppy.
- Morkie dogs are considered to be an eternal puppy, keeping their puppy-like appearance and behavior far into adulthood.
- They are companion dogs and are very loyal and love being with you. With your Morkie puppy, you will have found your best friend.
- Morkies love cats and quickly become friends with them. So if you have a cat, don't worry--they will soon be playing nonstop together and cuddling together during naptime.

Cons

- Morkies are very small and their size makes them fragile and defenseless. Care is needed when handling them. They are not recommended for families with small children. Young children often play roughly and could accidently drop your Morkie, causing a fracture.
- Morkies are ill-suited as guard dogs because of their size. They can bark and maybe bite around the ankles but that's about all. Also, the friendly disposition of Morkies doesn't make them cautious about strangers.
- All dogs, crossbred or purebred, will have some health problems. It is important to know the future concerns to take preparative measures now.

- Morkies are considered to be high-maintenance because they need to be brushed daily and bathed every three weeks to prevent their skin from drying out.

As you can see, the pros outweigh the cons, and the cons are not deal-breakers. Deciding to have a Morkie will be one of the best decisions of your life, as it will quickly become your best friend and faithful companion.

Adopting an older Morkie

Each year, many Morkies end up in shelters or are rescued from abusive families. These sad Morkies are in dire need of someone to adopt them and give them a loving home.

So how do you go about adopting a Morkie in need?

Use the Internet to search for a Morkie in your area. There are many websites that allow you to search based on your personal preferences, for instance, dogs that have been previously housetrained or dogs at

Photo Courtesy of
Brooke Durnell

shelters within a specified distance from where you live. Many animal shelters have websites that can direct you to rescue groups in your area.

When adopting a Morkie, here is a small list of questions that you can ask before you fall in love with your puppy:

1. Does it socialize well with other animals?
2. How does it respond to shelter workers, children, visitors, etc.?
3. How old is it?
4. Is it potty trained?
5. Has it ever bitten anyone that they know of?
6. Does it have any health issues?

Wherever you end up acquiring your Morkie, make sure you have a contract with the seller, shelter or rescue group that clearly explains the responsibilities for both parties.

As soon as you adopt your puppy or purchase it from a reputable breeder, take it immediately to your veterinarian for a checkup. A good veterinarian will be able to quickly spot any future concerns or health problems. The vet can also help you set up a regimen to keep your puppy in good health for years to come.

Never adopt a dog out of pity; only adopt a dog based on your energy level and compatibility!

Morkies and other dogs

Photo Courtesy of
Mary Tupper

Morkies are very social dogs and generally love other dogs and pets, whether they have been raised with them or not. Surprisingly, most Morkies love cats.

In most families there is some form of sibling rivalry. Parents often have to step in and put a stop to jealous and competitive behavior before it gets out of hand. You can expect a certain amount of sibling rivalry between your older pets and your Morkie when you bring it home. But the key is stopping it before it gets out of hand and becomes a habit.

Vaccines and other dogs

Puppies are normally vaccinated when they are four months old. It is recommended to avoid socializing with other dogs if you don't know with certainty that they have been vaccinated and are healthy for your little baby puppy.

Is it safe to introduce my puppy to my older dog?

If your adult dog is up to date on vaccinations, the chances of introducing an infection to either dog are remote. If you have an unvaccinated dog that is already sick, it could make your puppy very sick.

Ideal habitat for a Morkie

For as long as human history goes back, it has recorded dogs as companions for humans. Dogs are happier with human companionship, and humans are happier with canine companionship. Most dog breeds that exist today cannot survive without human companionship. They are unable to live in the wild or on the streets without someone filling their needs for shelter, warmth, food and love.

Companionship

As we have previously learned Morkies are very social dogs and they form a tight, inseparable bond of union with their owners. Their main goal in life is to please their owners and make them happy. You will find that your Morkie will cling to you from the minute you bring it home.

Your Morkie will be the most faithful and loyal dog you will ever have and all it will ask in return is your love and attention.

Dogs adapt to the environment where they live. If there is yelling and a tense atmosphere, your dog will likely avoid spending time with you. Try to make your home a peaceful haven not just for you and your family but also for the welfare of your Morkie.

Shelter

Your home is the ideal habitat for your Morkie because it is a warm, cozy and comforting environment. The main reason your home is ideal for your dog is because you live there.

Morkies don't require too much space, so they are happy living in a small apartment or having a small yard. The most important thing for them is feeling safe and secure because of your presence.

Morkies need to be with you and not locked in the laundry room or in a crate. If your lifestyle means you will be leaving your Morkie alone for hours at a time on a daily basis, maybe you shouldn't consider getting a Morkie. They are prone to suffering from separation anxiety, which can cause them to create mayhem throughout your house.

Food

Morkies are incapable of providing for themselves. They need you to cater to their nutritional needs daily. You will need to provide a healthy, wholesome diet and fresh water.

Some smaller dogs have a tendency to have food allergies, so you might need to adapt its diet. You will also need to watch your

Photo Courtesy of Harrison Rotker

Morkie's weight. Indoor dogs sometimes eat out of boredom, and can quickly gain weight.

You wouldn't feed your children food that contains a list of ingredients that you can't even pronounce every day, so why would you feed it to your dog? If you buy commercial food, make sure you know what you are buying. Choose wholesome healthy food that uses real ingredients and not just fillers and chemicals.

Love

Just like humans, all domesticated animals respond to love. Love makes us feel safe and secure. We know what makes us feel loved, but how can you show your Morkie that you love it?

Ear rubs are a great way to show your Morkie some affection. When a dog getting an ear rubs looks like it is high on love that is actually exactly what is happening: the ears are full of nerve endings that release endorphins when you rub them, making your dog feel loved.

Feeding your dog by hand is an intimate way of bonding with it, especially when it is a puppy. It communicates that you care about it and that you approve of its behavior.

You can also simply tell your dog that you love it. It might not understand your words but it understands the tone of your voice.

Is a Morkie puppy for you?

This chapter teaches us what the ideal family for a Morkie looks like. If you have a warm heart with lots of love to share, then a Morkie could be for you. They don't need much space and are very happy living in apartment buildings if you take them for frequent short walks.

We also learned how we could successfully introduce our little bundle of joy to our other dogs. We need to take into consideration their territorial instincts and introducing by their sense of smell.

Morkies are also a great choice for first-time dog owners. They are very easy to train and aim to please. They thrive with families that are elderly or with older children that will handle them carefully.

Morkies love to cuddle and are very sensitive to their owners needs. Do you appreciate a good cuddle and can you give your Morkie the companionship they need? If so, then a Morkie is the dog for you.

Does this sound like the dog for you?

Morkies will steal your heart in a matter of seconds and you will understand why they are rapidly becoming one of the world's most popular dogs.

Where should you buy your Morkie?

Once you have decided that you want a Morkie, it's tempting to try to get one as soon as possible. It's important, though, to do your homework and make sure your puppy comes from a reputable breeder and not a puppy mill. We've all heard the term "puppy mill" and probably know that it is associated with inhumane treatment of dogs, but what exactly do they do?

Puppy mills are also referred to as next-day pets. A puppy mill is a breeding facility whose goal is to breed dogs at the lowest cost possible while making the highest profit.

They use substandard breeding processes and inbreeding, which can lead to serious health and behavioral problems in the puppies bred there.

Since 1980s the Humane Society of United States has been trying to close down puppy mills, but sadly more and more keep popping up. But we can all do our part, by thoroughly researching before adopting or purchasing a puppy. Here are some helpful hints to avoid adopting from a puppy mill:

How to choose a respectable breeder:

- Avoid breeders that are only concerned about how soon you can take the puppy away and if your credit card or PayPal went through.
- Avoid pet stores, newspaper ads and too-good-to-be-true deals online. Many puppy mills supply false information that can end up costing you thousands of dollars in veterinarian bills.
- Ask your veterinarian about reputable breeders in the area.
- Avoid websites that advertise multiple litters available immediately or "puppies always available". Quick purchases are very convenient but are almost never from a reputable breeder.
- Remember: the best things in life take time. It will take time to find the right breeder for your Morkie and then you might have to wait until there is a litter.
- Look for a breeder that doesn't breed dogs until they are at least two or three years old.
- Say no to a puppy whose parents are unfriendly, won't let you approach them or growl at you, or if any of the puppies in the litter do any of those things. Bad behavior is learned from the parents.

The Humane Society of United States recommends that you put as much effort into researching where to buy a Morkie as you would when buying a vehicle or an appliance.

Before purchasing your Morkie, you will need to research the health of both parents. If possible, make sure both parents have a health clearance from the Orthopedic Foundation for Animals for patellar luxation (an issue with the kneecaps).

Also, do a background check with the Canine Registry Foundation, to certify if their eyes are healthy and normal. Most reputable breeders will show you a DNA test performed on the parents for progressive retinal atrophy.

Most serious health problems do not manifest until the Yorkshire terrier and Maltese have reached full maturity, which is between two to three years of age. Any reputable breeder will not even consider breeding their dogs until they have reached full maturity, as they will not have received the health clearances necessary before that time.

Just remember, Morkies will reflect the personality of their parents. A Morkie from an irresponsible breeder is likely to be a mess of the combined genetic problems of its ancestors--a whiny, noisy little tyrant of a dog that would be almost impossible to train and would likely also have a long, expensive list of health problems.

CHAPTER THREE

How to prepare your house for your Morkie puppy

Your Morkie will be a big part of your life and that means it will be with you 24/7. In the United States, more than 90 percent of household pets live indoors with their owners and your Morkie will be no exception. Morkies are extremely dependent on their owners and don't do well being left alone or confined to a separate area of the house. Once your Morkie has been successfully potty trained and taught to respect your things, it will need to have free run of the house.

To some people, the idea of a puppy loose in the house sounds like a recipe for disaster, with so many things just waiting to be broken or chewed to pieces.

It can be helpful to think of bringing your puppy home the same way you would think of bringing a toddler over for a visit. Would you leave things the way they are? Depending on your home, you would probably take the time to move some things out of harm's way, both to protect your belongings and to prevent injury to the child.

How to puppy-proof your home

All puppies, including your innocent-looking Morkie, have the ability to sniff out trouble in a matter of seconds. Dogs, in general, will investigate their new surroundings by smelling and tasting them. Your Morkie has inherited this natural instinct for exploring and investigative techniques.

When you bring your Morkie home, it will be fascinated with all the new smells and new hiding places. If precautions are not taken beforehand, your belongings can be destroyed in a matter of seconds, or even worse, your little Morkie can get hurt.

Whether your Morkie is a recently weaned puppy or an older rescued dog, it will love to explore. Many household items could be dangerous or even fatal if swallowed.

A basic rule of thumb for your adorable Morkie is to keep anything away from it that you would keep away from a toddler. Below is a list of potentially dangerous items that you will need to keep away from your Morkie.

Trash

Your Morkie's incredible sense of smell makes the odors proceeding from your trashcan too great of a temptation to resist. But the trash is filled with harmful bacteria and other items that could cut or even kill a puppy. A romp in the garbage could lead to a pretty hefty veterinarian bill.

If your trashcan is in plain sight, make sure it is too heavy for your Morkie to push over and has a tight lid on it. This way, if it does accidently get knocked over, the trash won't be spilled everywhere, allowing your Morkie to feast on a pile of garbage.

Electrical outlets and cords

Dogs and puppies can be strangely fascinated with electrical outlets, and may even try licking them. As for electrical cords, they may look to your puppy like slithery snakes that need to be chewed to pieces.

It's not hard to imagine the dire consequences if your little Morkie licks or chews on an electrical outlet or cord.

Before bringing your Morkie home, invest in some covers for your outlets and make sure all electrical cords are out of sight or secured against the wall. This will prevent your Morkie from having the (literal) biggest shock of its life.

Furniture and other decor

Photo Courtesy of Kevin Levesque

As mentioned above, Morkies love to explore by chewing and tasting everything in their sight and that includes your furniture. Especially when they are teething, chewing on items like your pillows, shoes or table legs can be very soothing on their sore gums.

Later we will cover how to teach your puppy not to chew on your furniture and other decor, but before you bring it home, it's important to think about how to prevent this from happening in the first place.

Before bringing your Morkie home, move any ornaments or decorations it might be tempted to chew on. Keep all of your shoes in a closed closet; all dogs love the smell of leather and those exotic stinky smells proceeding from your shoes.

Secure any lamps that you have sitting on tables that might fall to the floor when you are playing with your puppy. Pick up any baskets or other items that normally sit on the floor and put them away until your Morkie is correctly trained.

Also secure any dangling blinds and curtain cords so they are out of reach. This is one of the biggest dangers for all dogs and young children that many homeowners don't take into consideration. They can easily become entwined in the cords and choke themselves.

Another simple reminder: keep your toilet lid down. Besides being good etiquette, it will prevent your Morkie from accidently jumping in there and drowning.

Medication

Your puppy may not be able to tell the difference between your pills and its treats. Those sharp puppy teeth can easily chew the child-proof lid off a pill bottle, allowing your Morkie to devour the contents in record time.

Make sure you safely put away medications and toiletries before you bring your Morkie home.

Cleaning supplies

Puppies are extremely curious and they can't tell the difference between toxic chemical cleaning supplies and something non-toxic. Even if your puppy is put off by the smell, it could accidently knock something over onto itself and then try to lick the mess clean. This could have fatal consequences.

Before bringing your Morkie home, make sure all of your cleaning supplies are put in an area that it will not be able to access.

Household plants

Many new pet owners don't realize how curious a new puppy can be. They will try to smell and taste everything in their sight, including your houseplants.

Many houseplants are toxic for dogs, such as philodendrons, lilies, mistletoe and even tomato plants. If you are unsure whether your plants are poisonous for dogs, ask your veterinarian.

Before bringing your Morkie home, make sure all your plants are out of reach. Chewing on the leaves of the plants mentioned above could cause serious illness or even be fatal.

Backyard

Your Morkie's favorite place in the world will be your backyard, as it offers an endless selection of exotic scents and places to explore.

Before you bring your Morkie home, make sure there are no small holes in the fence that it could slip through. Morkies are extremely small so they don't need a very big opening to escape. Secure your fence and make sure there is nothing sharp or dangerous.

Stairs and balconies

Stairs can put unneeded stress on your Morkie's small, fragile developing bones. Making it walk up and down stairs can cause permanent damage to its hips and knees.

If you have a stairwell or stairs, make sure there is a gate in place to prevent your Morkie from going up or down the stairs. This will also keep it from accidently falling and fracturing a bone. Close off access to any balconies or high decks that your Morkie could easily fall through.

Compost

Compost piles are a smelly temptation for your puppy. If you have a compost pile in your backyard, make sure your puppy can't get to it. This is especially important if you are throwing your coffee grounds into your compost pile, as coffee grounds contain caffeine and even a small amount of caffeine is extremely toxic for all dogs.

How to prepare your house for the arrival of your new Morkie?

Above are some simple suggestions on how to prepare your house for your new puppy. By taking the time to puppy-proof your apartment or house, you will have peace of mind that your newly found four-pawed best friend will be safe and sound.

One of the best ways to check your house for potentially dangerous items is to get down on your knees and crawl through your house. This will allow you to see your house from your puppy's level. If you are unable to get on your knees, you can use your cell phone on a selfie stick the same way. Turn it on to video and walk through your house filming everything from below your knees.

A few days before you bring your new Morkie puppy home, give your house or apartment a thorough cleaning and double-check for any items that are break-able or chewable at puppy level.

House rules and routines

Could you imagine a family without rules and a set routine? Children thrive in families where there are rules and a well-established routine. It provides peace and a feeling of belonging for all the members of the family. The same applies to your Morkie puppy.

The minute you bring your Morkie into your house, it is trying to figure out how it fits into its new family. Consistency is the key for your Morkie to settle in and begin to feel like part of your family.

We all want our relationship with our dog to be based on mutual trust, love and respect. To gain that, we need to avoid harsh verbal and physical punishment. As we previously learned, Morkies are very sensitive. They get uptight and nervous when they are yelled at or treated badly, causing them to have deep emotional issues later on in life.

Golden rule: Treat your Morkie as you would like to be treated. Would you appreciate being treated differently every day, never knowing what is right or wrong? One day you are allowed on the couch; the next day

Photo Courtesy of
Anna Kaczor

you aren't. It would make you become agitated and confused. You show your puppy love and respect by establishing rules and sticking to them.

Before bringing your Morkie home, make sure your whole family is in agreement with the house rules for the new puppy. Discuss the following points with your family and make sure you are all on the same page.

Where will your Morkie sleep?

It is recommended that your Morkie sleep in a confined space, close to you. You can use a crate or box with the door open, which will create a den-like atmosphere, making your Morkie feel safe and secure. Morkies are very social dogs and can easily become stressed out when left alone.

Will you allow your Morkie on the furniture?

By cuddling with your Morkie on the couch, you are teaching it that being on the couch is good behavior that gets rewarded with a warm cuddle. If you decide to let your Morkie on the furniture, make sure everyone in the household is in complete agreement.

Some dog owners teach their dog to get permission before being allowed on the couch. This is a good habit to teach, especially if you often have guests that don't appreciate a dog trying to sit on their laps.

A word of caution: If you decide to let your Morkie sit on the couch, never allow it to jump onto or off of the couch as this can cause damage to its bones that can lead to future health issues. Pick it up to put it on the couch and to put it on the floor.

Where and with whom will your Morkie be during the day?

Morkies are very social dogs and have a tendency to suffer from separation anxiety when left alone for long periods. It will need to have company during the day.

If you work all day, see if it is possible to bring your little Morkie to work. The ideal situation for your Morkie and you is if you are retired or work from home. If that isn't possible, you might want to consider hiring a doggie sitter that drops in throughout the day, to check in on your Morkie and take it out for potty breaks.

What games will you allow your Morkie to play?

Not all games enforce positive behavior and some can actually encourage bad behavior such as jumping, chewing, biting and barking. Before choosing a certain game to play with your Morkie make sure it doesn't encourage these types of behavior. Be sure the entire family understands what games they are allowed to play with your Morkie and which ones are not allowed.

Who will feed your Morkie, what will it eat, and when?

Your Morkie will depend on you for all of its nutritional needs and regular feeding times. Just like you, it needs to have a regular eating schedule. It will need to eat four times a day until it is four months old, and then from four to twelve months, it will need to eat three times a day. Once it is over a year old, it will only need to eat twice a day.

You will need to decide on a feeding schedule before you bring your Morkie home. Also, you will need to decide who will be feeding it at the different times during the day. This will help to prevent overfeeding or forgotten meals.

Another important factor to decide before you bring your Morkie home is the type of food you will be feeding it. If you opt for commercial pre-made food, make sure it is made from whole foods and

Photo Courtesy of
Noki Barron

doesn't contain artificial preservatives. If you opt for a homemade dog food, make sure that you have food constantly on hand to feed your adorable little Morkie.

Who will be the main trainer for your Morkie?

Dogs have descended from wild wolves, so their basic instincts go back to the den. In a wolf den, there is only one leader. For this very reason, it is smart to choose only one main trainer for your Morkie; normally it is the person that will feed your Morkie on a regular basis.

Even though there will be one main trainer, everyone in the family can take part in potty training and other types of obedience training for your Morkie. It needs to feel like it is part of the family.

Before bringing your Morkie home, as a family, decide beforehand the tricks and behavior that you want your pup to learn. Make a list of the keywords to be used for reinforcing good behavior, so everyone knows the same good behavior cues, such as "Go potty".

How will your Morkie be corrected for bad behavior?

Permissiveness is every dog's worst enemy.

Make sure the whole family understands how to correctly discipline your Morkie. Never, ever use physical force to discipline your Morkie. Instead, when it makes a mistake (which it will), calmly interrupt your Morkie's bad behavior with a firm but kind "No" and then direct its attention to something else. Once it is behaving correctly, reward the good behavior.

Make sure the entire family understands that the goal is to replace bad behavior with good behavior.

Puppies learn their future habits during the first few weeks of their life with their owners. The key is not to give your Morkie the chance to chew on your cushions (or develop other bad habits). That way it will never know what it is missing later.

Having a pet is one of life's biggest joys but it comes with lots of responsibility. Taking the time and energy to correctly teach your Morkie the house rules will lead to a happy life together. Its behavior as an adult will reflect your teaching skills, so take the time now and teach it right the first time.

Supplies to have on hand

Parents awaiting the arrival of their new baby need months to pre-pare. A new puppy doesn't require as much preparation as a baby, but it does require a certain degree of organization before the big day when you bring home your Morkie puppy.

How can you make your Morkie as comfortable as possible as it settles into a new home away from everything it has ever known? What supplies do you need to have on hand in your home before your Morkie gets there?

- **Collar and leash**: You will need to choose one of the smallest collars on the market for your Morkie. Later on, you can buy another collar when it has finished growing. The collar should have a place to attach your Morkie's ID and license. How can you tell if the collar fits? You should be able to put two fingers under the collar and it shouldn't be able to slide over your puppy's head. The leash should be sturdy and well made. It should be at least four feet long. When your Morkie grows bigger and has been leash trained, you can invest in a longer leash.

- **Crates or puppy den**: If you have decided to crate train your Morkie, make sure it will have enough room to sit, stand and turn around in the crate, and also space for its food and water dish.

  If you will be using a puppy den alone or combined with a crate, you will need an expandable gate and a small covered area (a crate or a box) for your puppy to sleep in.

- **Bedding**: Your Morkie is used to the warmth of its mother and brothers and sisters for sleeping, so it will need to have a nice, soft, comfy blanket or cushion for sleeping on. You can find some excellent options at your local pet store that will keep your Morkie toasty warm while it is sleeping. It is recommended to choose a bed that is made with warm fleece or sheepskin.

- **Food and water dishes**: Avoid choosing dishes that are made from plastic; instead, look for dishes that are made from glass, ceramic, or stainless steel. Many plastic bowls contain dyes that can irritate your Morkie's eyes. Make sure you have the bowls filled up and ready to go on the day you bring your new puppy home, as it is likely be starving and thirsty after the long journey to your house.

- **Food and treats**: Even though your Morkie is tiny, it will have a huge appetite. Growing puppies need a healthy diet. Make sure to review the dietary recommendations for your Morkie with your veterinarian, to make sure the food you choose is suitable for your Morkie.

- **Grooming supplies**: Your Morkie will need to be brushed daily. The sooner it gets used to being brushed, the better it will behave when being groomed. You will need to choose a good quality brush designed for the type of fur your Morkie has. Brushing helps to keep your pup's skin and fur healthy and shiny.

- **Toys**: All puppies go through a teething period. It's normal for them to want to chew everything in sight because it soothes their sore gums. If you don't have some good quality chew toys on hand, you might as well say goodbye to your cushions, table legs and shoes.

  You can find a wide variety of chew toys at your local pet supply store. When your puppy is chewing on these toys, carefully monitor them and discard any toys that are getting worn out or destroyed. One of the most popular dog toys is the famous Kong toy that you can put treats inside and they fall out once in a while.

- **Cleaning supplies**: It is extremely important that you invest in high quality cleaning supplies for cleaning up after your puppy's bathroom messes. These cleaners will make potty training a hundred times easier.

Photo Courtesy of
Sam Hackbarth

At your local pet supply store, you can find many products that are considered to be pet-safe. When choosing a cleaner, look for products that contain enzymes, which will eliminate the scents that tell your dog to go the bathroom at the same spot. No odor means no future accidents.

- **Litter box and doggy litter (optional):** If you will be litter box training your little Morkie, make sure you have all the needed supplies on hand from day one. Make sure you have plenty of newspaper on hand, as you will need to make the transition from the newspaper to the litter box, little by little. Avoid using kitty litter as puppies will try to eat it and kitty litter is toxic if consumed.

Photo Courtesy of Melanie Levesque

Service providers

There are a number of service providers you may need to help meet your Morkie's needs, such as the veterinarian, groomer, trainer (if needed), boarding kennel, pet sitter, dog walker or even a doggie daycare center. The sooner you start researching the different service providers in your area, the better, as they will be an essential part of raising your adorable Morkie puppy.

Where do you start?

1. One of the best places to find information on any type of service provider is online, by typing in the keyword in your preferred search engine. For example, say you are looking for veterinarians in your area, type in "veterinarian, your city's name".

   A list of links will come up with the different professionals in the area. Many websites offer referrals and reviews about many of the businesses.

2. The second and most popular option in searching for service providers is by word-of-mouth. By asking your friends, family and neighbors, you can receive a trustworthy answer about the opinions of those you trust. Ask your neighbors and friends whom they recommend for a certain service.

   Also, if you enjoy using social media, ask all of your followers online for a recommendation for a certain service. People will be able to tell you about their positive and negative experiences. This will allow you to choose the best service provider for the job at hand.

3. If your area still has yellow pages, scroll through the phonebook in search of the service you are looking for. Once you have a list of phone numbers, pick up the phone and try calling them. Ask if they are accepting new clients.

Once you have a list of service providers, it is time to begin calling them. Here are hints for helping choose the best service provider.

You will find that if the service provider is friendly on the phone, they will generally be friendly in person too. If they are unfriendly on the phone, the chances are they will not be nice to your little Morkie. Cross them off the list.

If the service provider passes the telephone test, it is time for a personal visit. Ask them if you can drop by to ask them some questions and see their work place.

When visiting them, carefully observe how all of the employees treat the human and canine clients.

- Do they treat them with respect and care?

- Do the dogs look relaxed and comfortable or do they seem terrified and stressed?
- Are the facilities neat and tidy? Is there an offensive odor?

Take notes and cross off the service providers that don't meet your expectations. You are paying for a service, so make sure you get what you pay for.

Once you have picked the service providers you will be using, make a list of them and place it in a visible area, such as on your fridge. If you have chosen your Morkie's veterinarian, call and set up the first appointment.

The journey home

Finally, the big day arrives when you get to pick up your Morkie puppy and bring it to its new home with you. You might be feeling thrilled, but this journey home can be very overwhelming for your new Morkie.

Just put yourself in your Morkie's paws; this is not an exciting day but a very sad day. You are taking it away from everything it has ever known: its family, home and familiar surroundings. All of these changes can cause a puppy to become stressed out and even a little depressed.

How can you make the trip home more peaceful for your Morkie?

Before picking it up

You need to be relaxed. Your puppy can pick up on your vibes, so if you are stressed out, it will be too. Make sure to take time off from work for the day you bring your Morkie puppy home. If you can, take the first week off from work to help potty training be more efficient. Or you can aim for the day before a long weekend or your vacation. This will allow your puppy to adapt to its new surroundings with you there to help.

A word of advice: The worst time to introduce a new puppy to your family is during the holidays, as the festivities will keep you from giving your puppy much-needed attention.

Ask a friend or family member to join you in picking up your new puppy. Make sure they can drive your car, while you take care of your new baby puppy.

Another good reason to have a friend or family member along for the ride is that they are an extra set of ears. They can listen to any instructions given on how to take care of your Morkie. It is easy to forget something with so much excitement happening.

Before heading over to the breeder, write out a list of questions you might have. If you have been in contact with the breeder via email, you can also email them the questions. You might want to ask about your Morkie's feeding schedule and other general care.

Before the big day, ask your breeder not to feed your Morkie the day you plan to pick it up. Many puppies experience carsickness the first time they travel in a car and an empty stomach makes it easier to deal with.

If you plan on bringing your Morkie home in a crate, make sure you drop the crate off with the breeder a few days ahead of time. This way, the breeder can slowly introduce your Morkie to its new den and it won't be so traumatic.

The big day: Picking your Morkie up at the breeder

Ask the breeder if it is possible to have a few days' worth of the food your Morkie is used to. A sudden change of diet can upset your pup's stomach or even cause it to lose its appetite. It helps to mix the new food into the old familiar food, slowly increasing the amount of the new food.

Collect all of the necessary paperwork. Make sure you receive an official adoption contract, along with any veterinary records or other documents promised by the breeder.

Arrive early to your appointment. Try and spend ten to twenty minutes just playing with your new Morkie. Introducing yourself to your puppy will help it to be more relaxed on the drive home, since it will at least be familiar with your smell.

Car ride time

Again, put yourself in your puppy's paws. This is its first time to even be in a car and see the world pass by at such a fast pace. Let it explore your car before driving away. Puppies want to smell and investigate everything. This might take a couple minutes but it is all part of the trust process and you want your Morkie to trust you.

If possible, sit in the back seat with your Morkie and let your friend drive the car. Cover your lap with a blanket, just in case your Morkie gets a little carsick on the journey home.

If your puppy begins to cry or whine, don't be overly concerned and affectionate as that will just reinforce the behavior. Just pet it softly and try to help it relax. It will likely be so exhausted from playing with you and exploring your car that it will just go right to sleep.

If your puppy becomes unruly and noisy, place it on the floor between your feet. This will create a den-like area, which will make it feel safe.

If it is a long trip home, you will need to stop for frequent bathroom breaks. When choosing a spot for your baby Morkie to use the bathroom, make sure it hasn't been used recently by other dogs. Your little guy hasn't been vaccinated yet, so it can contract infectious diseases and also be a threat for other dogs.

Upon arrival at your Morkie's new home

Now it is time to introduce your adorable little Morkie to its new house. Since it will not be a temporary guest but a long-term resident, you want your puppy to feel at home. First impressions last the longest, so make sure your puppy feels relaxed and at ease while exploring its new surroundings.

Do not be quick to punish your Morkie during this investigating and exploring; this time will just add to its stress.

What should you introduce your puppy to first in its new home?

1. Take it to the designated area that you have already picked out for it to use for the bathroom. It most likely will have to go to the bathroom after the long car ride. If your puppy goes to the bathroom in its designated spot, praise it and give it a treat! It is never too early to start potty training your Morkie.

2. Next, bring your Morkie indoors to its water and food dishes. Make sure there is some food and water in the dishes, so it can help itself, if desired.

3. Now you can show it the sleeping area. If you are crate training, just leave the door open so it can go in and out.

Let your puppy explore the rest of your house freely, but watch it like a hawk. If it begins to chew on your furniture, quickly distract it and offer a chew toy instead.

Whenever your puppy looks at you, say its name in a cheerful manner. This will teach it two things: its name and that you are the pack leader. Your new Morkie will begin to settle in and soon be part of your family and home.

Introducing your Morkie to other pets

The key to introducing your older dogs to your new Morkie lies in introducing them the correct way for dogs and not humans. As humans, we rely on vision for meeting new people, but dogs rely mainly on scent.

You need to understand how your older dog may react to meeting a new dog; this will help you handle an aggressive reaction correctly. Often, pet owners can make these introductions worse because they freak out. What can you expect from your older dog?

Your older dog is not likely to welcome your new puppy with open paws. It might growl, snap or snarl at the little puppy, but almost never will it hurt the littler, younger dog. Dogs act this way because their territorial instincts come into play when their owners introduce a new dog into their house.

These territorial instincts are the main reason your dogs need to meet each other on their own terms and not ours. It is best if they can smell each other before the actual face-to-face meeting.

How can you introduce your dogs by using their sense of smell?

By following these four simple suggestions:

1. **First introduction**: Put each dog in a separate room or in their crates in different rooms with an object such as a blanket or toy that belongs to the other dog. The dogs feel very safe in their enclosed areas, but are allowed to smell the scent of the other dog without feeling intimidated. After a short time, switch these articles back to the original owners, so they can communicate by smell.

2. **Second introduction:** Let the new dog roam around the house. This allows it to take in its new surroundings and smell the new environment. It will be able to smell the other dog's scent around the house. While the puppy walks around the house, it is leaving its own scent

Photo Courtesy of
Jill Citron

around for the older dog to smell. It is very important during this step that the older dog is out of sight. After putting the new dog away, bring out the old dog, so it can smell the new scent.

3. **Third introduction:** Switch up the dogs. Take each one to the other dog's resting place and let them rest there. Also, when you take the dogs outside to use the bathroom, let each one smell the area where the other normally goes to the bathroom. This is quality scent time.

4. **Fourth introduction:** Finally, it's the big moment when they meet face-to-face. For territorial reasons, it is preferable to have the meeting on neutral ground. Perhaps, you can use a neighbor's backyard (or any enclosed area that is free of their scents). As they have already been formally introduced by scent, normally they will just run up to greet and smell each other, with no signs of wanting to fight.

This is the most stress-free method for introducing your dogs, mostly because you are showing respect for their natural instincts by using their sense of smell. You can do the above process in one day, but it works better over a series of days.

You need to remember that your house belonged to your older dog first and it has certain rights as the chieftain. How would you feel if some stranger just walked into your house without your permission? Most likely you would freak out and make the stranger leave your house, even if it meant using force.

Now imagine how your older dog feels. There is a strange dog in the house and its human parents are giving the new dog all the attention. Your older dog has the right to be upset and frustrated, so you need to be patient and remember that it will need extra reassurance that you still love it and are not replacing it with a newer dog.

Dogs communicate verbally, as we do, but they do so by growling and snarling. Your little puppy is still learning how to communicate and understand what your older dog wishes to say. Many times, new puppies miss subtle signals such as your older dog walking away or curling into a ball. Your older dog has to growl at your little puppy to get the message through, telling the puppy that it wants to be let alone.

If your older dog growls at your Morkie, don't be quick to punish the behavior. The growl is your dog's way of communicating and it is a sign for you that your pup should be separated for a short time.

It usually takes about three weeks for an older dog to accept the new dog. But just as not everyone in your family is going to be your exact cup of tea, you cannot expect your new dog to automatically be your older dog's best friend. Sometimes, your dogs will just tolerate each other as non-friendly roommates and other times, they will be best buddies.

Here are some helpful hints for what not to do when introducing your new Morkie to your older dogs:

- Do not hold your new dog in your arms while introducing it to your older dog. This will make the new dog feel insecure and helpless. Let the dogs meet at their own level, on the ground. You can be standing nearby, so the new dog can hide between your legs if it feels scared. But don't pick up the new dog until the introduction is completed.

- Do not let your older dog bully the new puppy. If it begins to act like a grumpy bully, it is time to separate the two of them for a while.

- Never lock the two dogs together in a room or crate, thinking they will work out their differences and become friends. How would you feel locked in a confined space with someone you didn't know? It is a recipe for disaster.

- Mealtime is sacred and all dogs' instincts come into play when it is mealtime. They need to protect their food. Never put meal dishes side by side; place them at on opposite sides of the room. By doing this, you will avoid fights and they will learn to only eat from their own dish.

- "Let them fight it out" is the worst advice in the world for both humans and dogs. Ask yourself: How do you feel about someone you had a verbal fight with? Do you feel like you worked out your differences or do you feel like there is more baggage in the relationship than before? Probably the latter.

Dogs might have short memories but allowing them to fight teaches them that that behavior is correct. The new dog will begin to feel bullied and insecure, leading to anxiety. Anxiety leads to behavior problems and difficulty with learning.

Make sure during the first two weeks after the initial introduction that you are always present when your dogs are together. You can leave them alone together once you are 100 percent positive that they have accepted each other.

A word of advice: It is important to continue with your older dog's normal routine, as it has certain habits and you don't want it to feel neglected. Make sure you feed your older dog, play with it and walk it at the same times you used to before you brought your Morkie home. This will help your older dog feel reassured that it hasn't been replaced by the newer dog.

CHAPTER FOUR
Potty training

Many dog owners dread potty training their dogs, but it can be a breeze if you follow the simple instructions found in this chapter.

Generally, it will take only one week to potty train your Morkie. The first couple days will require lots of time and energy, with each day getting easier and easier. Your Morkie might have an occasional accident after the first week, but this should be a rare occurrence.

Morkies, even though they are small, have a big appetite and an even faster metabolism. It is important for pet owners to realize that a Morkie will need more frequent trips to the bathroom than larger dogs.

What if you've adopted an older Morkie that still needs to be potty trained--will the suggestions in this chapter help your Morkie? Yes, they will, it just might take a little more time and effort on your part to teach your Morkie new good bathroom habits. It is possible to teach an old dog new tricks by using an extra dose of love and patience.

A word of advice before we begin the most important chapter in this book: Remember, your Morkie will respond to how it is treated. If you treat it with kindness, patience and an abundance of love, it will accept your training. But if you are nervous and agitated, your Morkie will become nervous and confused, which will lead to more accidents around your house.

Be prepared from day one

Benjamin Franklin once said: "By failing to prepare, you are preparing to fail."

It doesn't matter how many times you have heard that famous quote, read it again now and think about the endeavor you are about to embark on: potty training your Morkie. Your success with potty training depends almost 100 percent on how well you prepare for it before actually beginning. This whole chapter is dedicated to potty training your Morkie.

Here is a list of items for potty training that you should have on hand before you bring home your Morkie:

- **Treats:** Potty training and treats go hand-in-hand. Make sure you have plenty of doggy treats designed for your Morkie's age in your house, car and pockets before you bring your pup home.

  You won't have extra time for the first few days after your Morkie comes home to run to the store and get more. If you have opted to make homemade dog food and treats, make sure you made them up in advance and have your doggy biscuit jar and freezer full of snacks for potty training sessions.

  Treats will be used as a reward every time your Morkie goes to the bathroom in the designated spot. This teaches it that going the bathroom in a certain spot means being rewarded and getting treats, so it will repeat the process again and again, until it becomes a habit.

- **Squeaky toy:** You might be thinking: what does a squeaky toy have to do with potty training? It actually is very useful to stop your puppy from doing a dirty deed. If your puppy is about to go the bathroom on your carpet or floor, squeak the toy as a distraction to make it stop going to the bathroom. This will give you time to get it to the designated spot.

*Photo Courtesy of
Janine Tipton*

49

- **Litter box (optional):** This will be needed only if you will be litter box training your Morkie. When purchasing the box, make sure it is the correct size for a full-grown Morkie. Avoid choosing a box that has high sides, as it will be difficult for your tiny Morkie to crawl inside.

  Have the box ready to go, with litter inside and paper towels nearby, as puppies might have an accident before reaching the box. The litter should be designed for dogs and not cats, as cat litter is toxic if consumed by dogs. You will also need a pooper scooper to help with removing dried poop.

- **Baby gates:** Secure baby gates will prevent your Morkie from wandering into areas of your house where you don't want it to be until it is completely potty trained. Also, they can block off access to areas that could be dangerous for your little puppy, such as the stairwell or balcony.

- **Plastic bags:** Oblong bags, such as the ones used to cover newspapers, are ideal to use for picking up your Morkie's poop without getting your hands dirty. They can be found at almost every pet supply store or dollar store in your area.

- **Cleaning supplies:** Look for cleaning supplies that are designed to clean up puppy accidents. These cleaning supplies will be pet-safe and will destroy the invisible enzymes that are left behind when your puppy goes to the bathroom. These cleaning supplies can be found at your local pet supply store and most supermarkets. Make sure you have some paper towels for the initial cleanup and then to disinfect.

- **Leash and collar:** A leash will keep your puppy safely restrained from running away after its deed is done. Make sure your leash is at least four feet long, to give your Morkie space to move about in search of the perfect spot to go to the bathroom.

- **Doggie jacket or sweater:** This item is a must, if you will be potty training your tiny Morkie outside during the cold winter months. A sweater will keep it toasty warm and super cute while it takes its sweet time searching for the ideal spot to eliminate.

  If you want to step it up a notch, you can even get matching sweaters for your Morkie and yourself. Make sure you bundle up well too, before heading outside to take your Morkie to the bathroom. Morkies love to take their time in finding the perfect location for the bathroom. Also, investing in a large umbrella will keep your puppy and yourself dry on rainy days.

- **Black light (optional):** A black light helps you see all of the urine stains that are invisible to the human eye, making cleanup a breeze.

This will help you to clean up any accidents more efficiently to help prevent future mishaps.

- **Fencing:** If you have a backyard that you plan to let little Fido roam about in freely; make sure it is securely fenced off. It might help to get down to puppy level and make sure there are no holes or spaces that it can squeeze through to escape. Also, make sure that other dogs cannot get into your yard and hurt your itsy bitsy Morkie.

- **Crate (optional):** This will be a necessity if you will be using a crate for potty training your Morkie. Make sure the crate is the correct size for a full-grown Morkie to be able to turn around and lie down in it.

Before beginning, make sure you have the right attitude to keep potty training from turning into a long, drawn-out process. Here are some simple suggestions to make sure you have the correct attitude about potty training your Morkie:

Time plus patience:

Potty training your puppy doesn't happen by snapping your fingers. Successfully training your Morkie depends entirely on how much you are willing to put into it. At times, it will require you to be extra patient with your Morkie.

All puppies have very fast digestive systems: the smaller the puppy, the faster the metabolism. Morkies, being so small, have one of the fastest digestive systems of all dogs. This is actually to your advantage when potty training, since you know that shortly after eating or drinking your Morkie will need to go to the bathroom.

The first week, you will need to dedicate TIME to teach your Morkie to go the bathroom in the dedicated spot. Be prepared to run to the spot more than ten times a day the first week, as your puppy gets used to holding it in until reaching the spot and being rewarded. This will take time but it will be worth it in the long run, especially when you see your Morkie heading towards the designated spot on its own.

PATIENCE will be needed when you wake up in the middle of the night to a crying puppy that desperately needs to go the bathroom. It might be raining cats and dogs or below freezing outside as you wait for your Morkie to find the ideal spot to go the bathroom. Remember, this is just temporary; the first week, your Morkie is learning to control its bodily functions. Soon, it will be able to hold it in all night, without the need for a bathroom break.

Positive attitude

If you hover impatiently over your Morkie as it tries to go to the bathroom, it can become stressed out and nervous and might not even be able to go the bathroom. Then, when you go back into your house, it will have an accident because they just can't hold it anymore. Or the stress can make it spontaneously go to the bathroom wherever it is.

Remember, your stress and negativity rubs off on your Morkie. How well do you work with someone angrily looking over your shoulder?

When your Morkie is looking for the perfect spot to do its deed, don't add more pressure by telling it to hurry up or pushing it into the position. While your pup is looking for the ideal spot, be nonchalant and don't talk; just let it concentrate on the job at hand.

Some Morkie pups are shy about going to the bathroom in front of others, so you might have to look away and give them their privacy.

Some things in life just can't be rushed, so avoid rushing your Morkie to go to the bathroom. Try to enjoy the moment and see it as a time to bond with the world's cutest little dog.

If you feel like waiting for your puppy to go the bathroom in the designated spot is a waste of time, just remember, if you don't take the time to potty train now, your puppy will develop habits that will be very hard to break later on. You will be wasting more time in the future cleaning up messes. So relax; it's just a few days that will be tough.

The correct attitude for potty training your Morkie is to be:

- Patient
- Calm
- Persistent and consistent
- Positive
- Respectful
- Firm

Your Morkie is constantly observing your body language and tone of voice. If you have a bad attitude towards potty training your Morkie, it will pick up on this quickly and will most likely misbehave.

One of the best ways to have a patient and relaxed attitude towards potty training your Morkie is to take time off from work for the first few days after you bring your puppy home. If you are unable to take time off from work, you can hire a puppy-sitter to help with potty training when you are not there.

How to potty train your Morkie

Morkies have an extremely busy schedule with sleeping, playing, eating, going to the bathroom, and even more sleeping.

By understanding your dog's routine and habits, you will be able to potty train more successfully. We will discuss how puppy digestive systems work like clockwork, how they respond to routine, where to pick the designated spot and other helpful hints that will make potty training like a trip to the spa.

Clockwork

To begin, you need to understand how your puppy's little digestive system works. Five to twenty minutes after eating or drinking something, your Morkie is going to need to eliminate it. This is a key factor in potty training; by controlling its eating habits, you can control its bathroom habits.

Since it is still a puppy, it needs to eat more often during the day than larger dogs, because its tiny tummy can't hold much food and it has a faster metabolism than larger dogs. Morkie puppies need to eat about four times a day. Set up a regular feeding schedule around times when you will be home to take your puppy outside.

The Morkie's digestive system works like clockwork: what goes in must come out! Learn to work with your puppy's system and you might actually be lucky enough to not have any accidents in your house.

Routine

Morkies thrive on a well-established routine. From the very first day you bring your Morkie home, it wants to fit into your lifestyle and family. The sooner it understands the schedule and how it fits into the daily movements, the faster it will settle in, making potty training easier.

Stick to the eating, sleeping and bathroom areas you introduced your puppy to when you brought it home. Once it understands that everything has a place, potty training will make more sense. Avoid moving its bed and food dishes around daily.

Your Morkie will need to go to the bathroom more than eight times a day. Set up a routine that allows it to go to the bathroom about ten times a day and stick to that routine like glue.

Just before you go to bed at night, take your pup to the designated spot to go the bathroom. What if it is peacefully sleeping? Just pick it up and take it to the designated spot and wait till he does its deed. This is teaching it to adapt to your routine to avoid waking up in the middle of the night to a crying puppy that needs to go the bathroom.

Likewise in the morning, before making your cup of coffee, go wake your puppy up and take it to the designated spot to go the bathroom. It most likely will want to play with you, so be patient while it learns your schedule.

The first few days, you will probably have to be running to the designated spot every two hours, but little by little, the intervals will get longer, as your puppy's bladder gets bigger and stronger. Before you know it, your Morkie will be able to make it through the night without needing a bathroom break.

Potty training teaches your puppy that there is a set time and place for going to the bathroom. It cannot just go wherever and whenever it wants to--there is a time and place for relieving itself.

Pick the spot

Your Morkie needs to feel safe and sound in the designated spot. Make sure no big noisy vehicles are passing by, as this will frighten your Morkie and it won't go to the bathroom.

A word of advice: Pick a spot that hasn't previously been used by another dog. All dogs, including your Morkie, are fascinated by other dog scents and the smells can become so overwhelming that they quickly forget the reason you were outside was to go to the bathroom. Choose a spot that only your Morkie will use and it will only be able to smell its own scent there.

When you are choosing the designated spot, make sure that you can reach it quickly. Also, avoid choosing a spot that is directly outside of your door or porch, as it will continue to use that area, long after potty training is complete. As your Morkie continues to grow, so will the size of its poop--that isn't the first thing you want to see when you walk into your house.

Apartment buildings: If you leave in an apartment building, getting outside quickly can almost be impossible and you don't want your Morkie relieving itself in the elevator. What can you do?

As mentioned before, it is quite easy to litter box train your Morkie. You will still follow all of the suggestions found in this chapter, but just adapt them to make the litter box the designated spot.

Introducing your Morkie to the designated spot

When you bring your Morkie home for the first time, make sure the first place you take it is to the designated spot, whether outside or inside where the litter box will be. Most likely, it will be exhausted from the long journey home and will need to relieve itself as soon as possible.

Pick your Morkie up and carry it to the designated spot. Put it down and say, "Go potty". Your puppy won't understand exactly what you want, but it is the beginning of using a keyword for potty training. Let it check the area out, taking time to smell and investigate the area. If the designated spot is outside, it might want to play a little.

If your puppy doesn't go to the bathroom in the first 5 minutes, go inside and show it the bed and food dishes. Once it has checked out its new home, take it outside again to the designated spot. This time, don't go back inside until it has done its deed. This leaves behind the scent that tells it to go potty here. This scent will encourage it to repeat the potty process in the designated spot again, making potty training easier.

When should you take your Morkie to the designated spot?
- Whenever your puppy wakes up. (Morning, afternoon or evenings)
- Whenever it finishes eating or having a big drink of water.
- After playing or being excited.
- If you hear it whining at night or anytime of the day.
- If it is standing at the door looking to go outside.

Some more helpful hints
- Your Morkie will need to eat at least three times a day: breakfast, lunch and dinner. Make sure you feed it at the same time every day, as feeding times will affect bathroom times.
- Morkies will need to go the bathroom about ten times a day, on average. Normally they will need to go after eating, drinking, sleeping, or playing.
- Try to take your Morkie to the designated spot as much as possible. After it goes to the bathroom on the designated spot, make sure you generously reward the behavior with a treat and tons of praise.

General potty training schedule

This schedule isn't a rule, just a general idea as to how often you will need to take your Morkie to the designated spot. You can adapt it to your lifestyle and what works best for your Morkie and you.

Make sure you have a pair of shoes and some clothes to throw on, for midnight emergencies and to run out when you first get up in the morning. The first thing you should do every morning is to take your Morkie to its spot.

MORNING	
6:00 - 6:30	Take your Morkie outside IMMEDIATELY
7:15 - 7:30	Indoor playtime
7:30 - 8:00	Feed your puppy in its confined space. (Allow 15 to 20 minutes for digestion)
8:00	Take your puppy to the designated bathroom spot
8:15	Place puppy in its confined area
AFTERNOON	
12:00	Take your puppy outside
12:15 - 12:00	Indoor playtime
12:30 - 1:00	Feed your puppy in its confined space (Allow 15 to 20 minutes for digestion)
1:00	Take your puppy to the designated bathroom spot
1:15	Place your puppy in its confined area.
EVENING	
5:00 - 5:30	Take your puppy outside
6:15 - 6:30	Indoor playtime
6:30 - 7:00	Feed your puppy in its confined space (Allow 15 to 20 minutes for digestion)
7:00 - 8:00	Take puppy outside
8:00 - 9:00	Indoor playtime
9:00	Place your puppy in its confined area
10:30 - 11:00	Take your puppy outside

Morkies that are younger than four months will need to eat four times a day; if your Morkie is that young you will need to adapt the schedule.

Rewards and potty training

We all respond to being rewarded for good behavior. All puppies love rewards and will do almost anything to receive one.

Studies have shown that when animals are rewarded for good behavior, it sends a message to their brains telling them that it is beneficial to repeat this behavior. When they repeat the behavior and they are rewarded, the desire to repeat the behavior becomes stronger. After a while, it just becomes part of their normal routine and there will be no need to reward them for the behavior anymore.

This is the whole point with potty training. You want to teach your Morkie that going to the bathroom in a certain spot is a desired behavior. To do so, you need to send a message to its brain using treats and praise, so it will want to repeat the same behavior.

How and when should you reward your Morkie?

The reward needs to be given to your Morkie **immediately** after it relieves itself in the designated spot. Never wait till you get back into your house to give the treat, as your puppy will not be able to associate the treat with going to the bathroom. The reward process has to be immediate if it is going to be effective.

What are some different types rewards you can give your tiny Morkie?

Verbal rewards: To effectively give a verbal reward, get down to your puppy's level (if you can) and pet it generously, telling it at the same time how proud you are. Dogs can pick up on the positive vibes in your voice, so make sure you speak softly and transmit kindness in your tone of voice.

It can be extremely difficult to show this kind of enthusiasm at 2 o'clock in the morning, but remember this is only temporary. You will not need to take your Morkie outside to the designated spot past midnight very many times before it will learn to control its bodily functions.

Edible rewards: You can use a variety of treats for rewarding your pup when it goes the bathroom in the designated spot. This reward is the most effective way of teaching your Morkie good habits.

The best way to do this is to offer a treat at the same time you are giving your pup verbal encouragement.

If you are potty training an older Morkie and are concerned about extra weight gain from all of the extra treats, you can reduce the amount of food given at mealtime to compensate for the extra calories during potty training. Potty training an older dog can be a challenge but it can be done, especially if you are giving your dog its favorite treats.

Physical rewards: Physical rewards can be very gratifying bonding moments for you and your Morkie. A physical reward is when you begin to play with your puppy immediately after it uses the designated spot.

If you use all three of these types of rewards when your Morkie correctly uses the designated spot, it will actually want to use the bathroom spot.

The more your Morkie is rewarded for going the bathroom in a designated spot, the faster it will make the connection and be potty trained. This is why it is of utmost importance during the first few days of potty training. The first few days will set the pattern for the rest of your puppy's life.

To crate train or den train

Both crate training and den training involve confining your Morkie to a small space, blocking off access to the rest of your house. Crate training uses a crate with a closeable door, while den training gives your Morkie a small area in your house enclosed by an expandable gate.

All confined areas should be free from furniture and any other non-dog related items that could turn into chew toys.

If you opt to den train your Morkie, you can purchase an expandable exercise pen or playpen at most pet supply stores. This can easily be set up in any room in your house. It recommended for the first week of potty training to set it up on waterproof flooring, in case of accidents.

Inside the crate or the puppy den, place something soft and cuddly for your puppy to sleep on. Include water and food dishes, and a few of your Morkie's favorite chew toys.

How to get your Morkie to love its confined area:

Step 1: Take your Morkie outside for a walk or some serious playtime. This will get your little pup tired out, so it will be eager to go into the confined area.

Step 2: Once your Morkie is in the confined area, give it a stuffed Kong or some treats. This will keep it distracted as you go about your business in your house.

Step 3: Your puppy will probably finish the treats in about five minutes; this is when it will realize that you have abandoned it in this confined area. It might begin to whine or cry, but just ignore this until it stops. Once the whining stops, you can go make a fuss over your puppy.

Step 4: On day two, try leaving the house for a short period, such as going outside to water the plants or check the mail. As the days pass, leave the house for longer periods (only after your Morkie has already had a bathroom break).

Repeat steps 1-3 throughout the day, gradually increasing the amount of time you will be leaving your puppy there alone. You can start off with as little as one minute and gradually work up to twenty minutes or so.

Leave your puppy in its confined area for the night, but if you hear it barking during the night, get up and take it to the bathroom.

Clean the area immediately after any accident, to help prevent more accidents from happening.

Photo Courtesy of
Tami Mclaughlin

Crate training

The key to crate training your Morkie is to teach it that the crate is its den and it is a safe area. Basic instinct teaches dogs that things will go bad pretty fast if they start relieving themselves in their sleeping area.

Crate training involves confining your pup to its crate and closing the door anytime you aren't playing with it or feeding it. The crate is a tight, confined area, so your Morkie will catch on quickly that it is only for sleeping and not for going to the bathroom. It will want to keep its sleep area clean, so it won't go to the bathroom.

As mentioned previously, the crate should only be big enough for a bed and a water dish. Your Morkie should be able to stand and turn around comfortably inside of the crate, allowing for some growing room.

Once you have the ideal crate, you need to choose the ideal location for it. You can always move the crate around to where you are, but during the first week of potty training it is highly recommended to keep your Morkie in one place. Morkies are very social dogs, so much sure you choose a place that is close to you and the rest of the family.

Word of advice: Never place your Morkie in its crate under direct sunlight, as this can cause your pup to become overheated, leading to heatstroke and other complications.

Your Morkie's first introduction to the crate shouldn't be forced. Let it walk into the crate alone and explore it. Don't close the door right away, as that will just cause it to panic and hate the crate from that moment on.

If you need to bribe your Morkie to go into the crate, just place some treats inside the crate and it should follow the treats without even realizing it is inside the crate. Once it is inside of the crate, pet and praise your puppy, so it understands that being inside of the crate is a good thing.

Once your Morkie seems comfortable inside of the crate, try to close the door partially for short periods, while you are nearby. Slowly work up to closing the door completely.

If it begins to whine or bark to be let out, don't let it out or sweet-talk it. This is the moment that tough love comes into play. If you let your puppy out while it is crying, you are teaching it that whining is the code to be released from the crate.

Den training

Most Morkie owners want a lap dog, however, rather than leaving their pet locked in a crate most of the day. This makes den training a more popular method for potty training.

Den training teaches your Morkie that your whole house is its den for sleeping.

A puppy den limits your puppy's access to other parts of your house to reduce the amount of accidents that your puppy would have if it were given free run of your home. This prevents the spread of the scent that would redirect your puppy to use the bathroom repeatedly in the same spot, over and over again.

These puppy dens are just temporary confined spaces until your Morkie has been correctly potty trained. Make sure to keep the den and crate area very clean. Your puppy will understand that this is its private area and it is unacceptable to go to the bathroom in there.

Make sure the puppy den has a bowl of fresh water for your Morkie at all times. It will also need a food dish that will be used three to four times a day until it is about a year old. Make sure there are some toys inside of the den so your puppy doesn't get bored.

When you put your puppy in the puppy den, start by leaving it there for a short period. If it begins to cry or whine when you leave, don't quickly rush back to reassure it that everything is okay. This will just teach it that whining and crying is acceptable and that you will come running.

Many will combine a puppy den with crate training by using the crate as the sleeping area for their puppy. The door should be tied open, so that it wouldn't be able to close and lock your pup inside. Place it in the corner of the den to teach your puppy that the crate is its friend so it can be used in the future for travelling, etc. without causing your Morkie added stress.

Your puppy will understand from day one that this is its safe spot— its own special area that it will not want to stink up by eliminating there.

Is it cruel to confine your puppy to a small area?

In this day and age, everybody seems to have an opinion about everything, including how you potty train your dog. But you don't want to make a decision based on somebody else's strong opinions; you need to understand the whole picture.

Would you let your toddler roam freely about your house unsupervised and without diapers on, sometimes for hours at a time? Of course not! There are way too many opportunities for your baby to get hurt or get into trouble.

Now, let's think about your Morkie and your house. Even if you have puppy-proofed your house, it still offers your puppy an endless supply of bathroom spots.

As you recall, all dogs descend from wolves, and for the first few months of their lives, their mother keeps them in a den. Is she being overly confining and restrictive? No, it is part of the basic instinct that she uses to keep her pups safe and teach them not to go the bathroom inside of the den.

Confining your dog will only be necessary for the first seven days or so and it is the key to successfully potty training your Morkie. The first week is when you will teach it either good or bad habits. But why can we say it is wise to confine them to a puppy den?

- Confining your puppy is only a temporary measure and will not be used permanently; it serves the sole purpose of teaching it to control its bodily functions and not go to the bathroom except where it is supposed to.

- If you allow your puppy to roam about your house as it pleases, it will go to the bathroom wherever it happens to be, making more work for you and spreading its scent all over the place, which sends a message to its brain telling it to repeat its dirty deed in the same spot. It might seem innocent at first, but as your puppy grows, its urine gets stinkier and its poop gets bigger; plus, it is learning bad habits that will extremely hard to break later on.

- If you plan on leaving your Morkie home alone when it is older, but don't take the time to properly potty train when it is little, it will most likely wind up locked into a small crate when it is older. You won't be able to trust it to be left out in your house alone without using the bathroom everywhere. *Not confining your Morkie when it is little leads to longer periods of confinement when it is bigger.*

- The sad reality is that every year many cute dogs are euthanized because they were not properly potty trained.

So is it cruel to confine your Morkie for potty training? Clearly it isn't cruel because it is for its own well-being and will bring long-term benefits for both of you.

Make sure to set up the crate and puppy den before you bring your puppy home. This will instantly teach your puppy that this is its den and it needs to be kept clean.

Word of advice: Little accidents lead to bigger accidents. The key to potty training is to prevent the little accidents from happening.

Pros and cons of crate and den training

Pros of crate training

1. It provides you with peace of mind; especially if you have to leave your Morkie alone for hours. You will be able to trust it roaming about the house, without worrying about your oriental rug being used as a bathroom.

2. Crate training is an extremely effective way of potty training your puppy because it forcibly trains your Morkie to control its bodily functions fast. You can use the basic canine instinct of keeping sleeping quarters clean to your advantage.

3. Crate training is especially useful when potty training an older Morkie.

4. If you will be travelling with your Morkie frequently by plane or car, you will need to transport it in a crate and it won't be stressed out because it sees the crate as its den.

Cons of crate training:

1. Your Morkie learns that the crate is its den. It won't relieve itself inside of that crate, but the rest of your house is fair game. It might not fully understand its boundaries and could have an unwanted accident in your house.

2. Morkies, like all small dogs, can become more aggressive with children and unknown guests if they have been crate trained.

3. Quite a few people consider crate training to be a form of animal cruelty because the dog is locked into the crate and cannot escape. They reason that we would not lock a small child into a cage, so we shouldn't do the same with a dog.

4. Crate training is not suitable for all dogs, especially dogs that have spent a lot of time in a crate or cage (such as in a shelter or with previous owners) as it may make them very agitated and upset.

5. Smaller dogs can suffer from separation anxiety and being confined in a small space can make them very upset and stressed.

6. Crate training is not natural. It could be reasoned that dogs descended from wolves that live in dens. But wolves are able to leave their den at will. The crate limits your Morkie to an artificial confined area, which many pet owners use for their own convenience. If you do decide to use a crate, make sure you limit the time your Morkie is locked inside of it to what is absolutely necessary.

Pros of den training

1. Smaller dogs that are den trained as opposed to crate trained tend to be friendlier with children and strangers.
2. Morkies that are den trained are less likely to suffer from separation anxiety, as they don't feel claustrophobic and confined.
3. Den training teaches your Morkie little by little that your whole house is its den, so it will not eliminate in your house when left alone or wandering around unsupervised, once potty trained. By basic instinct it will keep its den clean from bathroom smells.
4. Den training is considered to be a very humane way of potty training because you allow your Morkie to move about and not be locked in a small cage.
5. Den training is considered to be one of the most effective ways to potty train smaller dogs, as they will typically be living inside with their owners. It teaches your puppy that the whole house is its den and it cannot go to the bathroom inside.

Cons of den training

1. Your Morkie could push over its barrier when left unsupervised and escape, finding a bathroom spot under your kitchen table.
2. Since the confinement area is larger than a crate, there might be one or two accidents within this area. This can be quickly cleaned up to avoid future accidents.

Clean-up advice

Accidents are going to happen, even with the world's best potty trainer. So don't fret about it. But the key to preventing future accidents is to understand the importance of why it is so important to clean up after them.

Basic instinct

The day your Morkie was born, its mother began to train it to be clean and keep the area around it clean. Morkies learn from that day forward that the den is for three things: eating, drinking and sleeping. Tiny puppies relieve themselves in the den but their mother quickly licks up any mess they make.

Their mother's basic instinct kicks in and causes her to be constantly tidying up the den and her baby pups. Their little space never smells like urine or feces. The pups are brought up knowing that their living quarters need to be free of messes. As the pups grow, they begin to move away from their sleeping area to go the bathroom. You want your Morkie to see your whole house as part of the den or living area.

When you bring your Morkie home, it doesn't understand where its sleeping quarters end and its bathroom area begins. All it knows is that it can't relieve itself where it sleeps. But how can cleaning up after your puppy contribute to potty training?

Enzymes

Have you ever noticed how dogs love to smell other dogs' pee? Once they have finished smelling the other dog's scent, they suddenly have the urge to go to the bathroom too.

Why do they do that?

All dogs have enzymes that are left behind in their urine and feces. These little enzymes are left behind, even if you wiped up the mess or the rain washed it away.

If these enzymes haven't been cleaned up correctly, your Morkie can smell them. These enzymes are telling it, "Go to the bathroom here, this is the perfect spot." This is the main reason why so many pet owners have repeat accidents on the same spot: the mess is gone but the enzymes are still there.

How can we eliminate these invisible enzymes?

The only way to remove these enzymes is by using heavy-duty cleaning products. You can find them at your local pet supply store or supermarket; they have been specially designed for cleaning up your pet's messes. These products will destroy or neutralize your dog's enzymes, so they stop inviting your dog to relieve itself inside of your house.

Word of advice: Avoid using cleaning products that contain ammonia. Ammonia makes the enzymes smell stronger and upon smelling it, your puppy instantly will want to go to the bathroom. This is why is your puppy will often have accidents on the same spot, over and over again.

To successfully potty train your Morkie, the key is cleaning up right after it has an accident.

If you are planning on using a litter box for potty training your Morkie, don't be too quick about changing the litter or removing fecal matter in the beginning. You want your puppy to recognize its own scent so it will reuse the litter box.

If you are training your Morkie to go to the bathroom outside, always take it to the same spot, so it won't get distracted by the scent of other dogs.

If you have another dog, make sure they each dog has its own litter box or designated spot outside. If they have to share spots, they will take a long time going to the bathroom, as they will need to investigate the scent left by the other dog.

How to correctly clean up after your puppy

1. Pick up the fecal matter or wipe up the urine with a paper towel. Place the paper towel into a garbage bag.
2. Spray a cleaning product designed for cleaning up after your puppy all around the area. The enzymes can be spread up to a foot around the mess, so be generous in cleaning up.
3. If your puppy accidently stepped in its mess, wipe off its paws with water. Do not use chemicals that could make it sick. Use a clean rag and the cleaning product for wherever it might have wandered.
4. If possible use paper towels for cleanup or a new rag for each spot, to avoid spreading the enzymes around the house yourself.
5. Be quick when cleaning up messes, especially if the mess was made on the carpet, as the padding underneath can quickly absorb it.

Dos and Don'ts in potty training

You will find the minute you tell your friends and family and you are getting a puppy, everyone suddenly turns in an expert on potty training. But not all the advice you will receive is helpful for potty training your Morkie.

Your tiny little Morkie is just beginning to learn to control its bodily functions. How would you treat a tiny baby, if it pooped its pants? You would lovingly clean up the baby, never scolding it because the baby is unable to comprehend what just happened. Remember that your Morkie is still a baby too and needs to be taught how to control itself.

The worst advice that you might receive is: Just rub your dog's nose in its mess; that will teach it not do that again. Rubbing your dog's nose in its mess is not going to teach it anything except that you are crazy. All dogs have short memories, so by the time you are rubbing its nose in the mess, your puppy has forgotten all about it.

Your Morkie is extremely sensitive and does not respond well to yelling and screaming. It causes agitation and stress, which will likely lead to loss of bladder control and another accident.

Morkies, like all dogs, can take awhile to find the perfect spot to go to the bathroom. Don't become agitated or visibly upset. It will make your puppy become nervous, and then it will forget that it had to go to the bathroom, so it won't go. Later, it won't be able to hold it in anymore and probably have an accident in the house.

Caught in the act

How should you react if you catch your Morkie in the act of going potty inside your house?

You need to understand that if you catch your dog doing its deed inside of your house, it is your fault. It is not your Morkie's fault that you didn't get it to its designated spot in time for it to go to the bathroom. Your Morkie has a very small bladder and just can't hold it in for very long periods.

There are some warning signs that can alert you to take your Morkie to its designated spot. You need to be able to identify these warning signs, in order to be able to prevent accidents from happening inside of your house. Here is a list of warning signs to watch out for:

1. All dogs and puppies love to smell and check out an area before they go to the bathroom there. So, if you see your Morkie pup intently smelling a certain area and beginning to go around in circles, it is time to pick up your puppy and take it to its designated spot.
2. If your puppy begins to squat that is a sure sign that it is about to go the bathroom. Quickly but gently, pick it up and hold it so that its belly is against yours to stop it from peeing. Take it to the designated spot, so it can go pee. If it went inside the house, it was your fault for not paying attention.
3. If your puppy begins to bark or whine while looking in the direction of its designated spot, it is probably trying to communicate with you and tell you that it needs to go to the bathroom now. Pay attention to your Morkie's verbal expressions.

Again, never ever get mad or yell at your Morkie if it has an accident in your house. If you feel the need to be upset with someone, be upset with yourself for not paying better attention to your Morkie and taking it outside before the accident happened.

If your Morkie is *already peeing,* quickly pick up your Morkie and say a firm "No". Then carry it to the designated spot, holding its tail between its legs to prevent it from urinating. Let it finish up peeing in the designated spot and then generously praise your puppy and give it a treat. When you go back inside, be quick to clean up the mess it started to make inside.

It is easier to stop your Morkie from going pee than going poop. If you notice your puppy getting in the position to go pee, try to startle it by using a squeaky toy, which you can squeeze just as it begins to pee. This will startle your puppy without frightening it. As all dogs are extremely curious, it will probably have to come and investigate the strange noise it just heard. This will give you the time you need to pick up your Morkie and take it to its designated area.

If your puppy is caught in the act of pooping, there is only one option: just let it finish its business. If you try to pick it up while it is going poop, you are only going to make a huge mess: on yourself, on your dog and in your house. Just let it finish and then clean up the mess.

Word of advice: When cleaning up the mess, don't make a big show out of it. Your Morkie already feels bad for what it did. Remember it is just a baby and accidents happen. Also remember that it was your fault because you didn't get it to the designated spot in time.

The number one rule when potty training your Morkie is: *If you don't catch your puppy in the act, don't punish it.* Don't even talk to your dog about the mess; just clean it up.

Whenever your Morkie successfully goes to the bathroom in the designated spot, take the time to reward it. It isn't necessary to reward with a snack every time; one of the best rewards is your praise and playtime with you. Take time to play with your puppy and tell it how proud you are after it goes to the bathroom.

You need your Morkie to associate rewards with good behavior, such as going to the bathroom on its designated spot.

Here are some moments when you should never praise or reward your Morkie:

- It was home alone and had an accident in the puppy den or crate.
- It was caught in the act but you didn't catch it in time to take it to the designated area.
- It escaped from the crate or puppy den and did its dirty deed in your house.

Never ever give any type of reward to your Morkie for bad behavior, as this will just reinforce bad habits.

Punishment

The best punishment for your Morkie is not being able to see your approval and not being praised for going to the bathroom. It will begin to connect the dots: praise comes from going in a certain spot and not from going inside the house. Avoid yelling and screaming when accidents happen, as it will cause your Morkie to become agitated and unable to distinguish right from wrong.

All dogs and puppies live in the moment and not the past. They're not meditating on the poop they did behind the potted plants and when their owner will discover it. It was done and forgotten about.

Your Morkie is a very intelligent dog but that doesn't mean it understands the difference between relieving itself behind the couch and relieving itself outside. Punishing your puppy for going to the bathroom inside your house doesn't accomplish anything beneficial, it just teaches it that it needs to distrust and fear humans.

For example: Your dog pooped on the kitchen floor while you were out. When you come home, you find it sulking in the corner, looking extremely upset.

Some people might reason that this behavior indicates that the dog knows it cannot poop inside of the house and is showing remorse by sulking.

But the truth of the matter is that your puppy is sulking in the corner because it associates your arrival with yelling and screaming. It has totally forgotten about relieving itself on the kitchen floor and is sulking out of fear of you. The only thing your Morkie understands is you being mad when you get home.

The key to successfully potty training your Morkie is to teach it that relieving itself in the designated spot makes you very happy. A Morkie's only goal in life is to please its owner.

Once you understand how your dog thinks, you will be able to avoid punishing it for things it doesn't even remember. We need it to understand why it isn't being praised for going to the bathroom. If it doesn't understand the reason behind the punishment, it will make potty training more tedious and slower.

When should you punish your Morkie for bad behavior?

The only time you should punish your adorable little Morkie is if you catch it in the act of going to the bathroom, not after the fact.

How should you punish it?

The punishment should only be a firm "NO" or "BAD PUPPY". Then take the puppy to the designated spot to finish up there. It should not receive any type of reward after finishing up its deed.

Never hit your puppy, yell, or rub your puppy's nose in its dirty deed.

Spontaneous peeing

Morkie pups and dogs have a tendency to lose control of their bladders when they get overly excited. It can happen while they are playing, greeting you, or meeting somebody new.

Don't punish your dog for spontaneously peeing. It can't control itself, and most likely, doesn't even realize that it just peed. As it gets older, spontaneous peeing will likely cease.

Litter training your Morkie

Normally when we think of litter boxes, we instantly think of cats. Most litter designed for litter boxes is called kitty litter and is designed for cats and not dogs. The good news is that it is becoming more popular to litter box train your dog and you can purchase doggy litter.

When should you consider litter box training your Morkie?

1. Many Morkie owners live in apartment buildings or condos that have no or limited access to a green area for their Morkie to relieve itself. It is more practical to have a litter box in the house for quick and easy access, which make potty training a breeze.

2. Morkie pups have small bladders. Having a litter box in the house gives them the freedom to go whenever they want to. Most Morkie owners that have litter boxed trained their pup have expressed that their puppy never had an accident in the house.

3. When your Morkie is litter box trained, wherever you travel, your Morkie will be fine as long as there is a litter box. You won't be waking up to an unwanted surprise on your host's rug.

4. Your Morkie can use the litter box when it is alone in the house. It will still go to the bathroom when you take him on walks outside (bring your pooper-scooper!), but it won't have to wait for a walk if it needs to go.

How can you train your Morkie to use the litter box?

1. In the confined area, place newspaper on the floor, with a small plastic tray under it to prevent leakage, if possible.

2. Place your puppy on the spot and say "Go potty." It may not go, but repeat the process by saying "Go potty," to help teach it that this spot is something positive.

3. You might need to soak the newspaper in your dog's urine from when it went to the bathroom outside, as the smell will send a message to its brain that it needs to relieve itself there.

4. Watch your puppy like a hawk and when you see it about to go the bathroom, quickly pick it up and place it on the newspaper. Again, tell it to "Go potty." Once it has gone on the newspaper, it will most likely go there again. Liberally praise it each time it goes potty on the newspaper.

5. Once it has gone three or four times on the newspaper, put some doggy litter on top of the newspaper. It should continue using this area for its bathroom, since its scent is telling it to return to this spot. Note that your puppy will most likely be wary of litter in the beginning. Repeat step 2.

6. Once your puppy is used to the litter and going to the bathroom with the newspaper and litter, you can bring out the litter box. Place the dirty newspaper at the bottom of the box and the litter on top. The scent and material will let your Morkie know that it is acceptable to go the bathroom here. Repeat step 2.

7. Once your puppy is used to the new box, you can move the box about a foot each day towards the area where the box will permanently stay in the future. Make sure the box has newspapers around it, as accidents might happen en route to the box. Be quick in cleaning up after them. Every time you move the box closer to the designated spot, repeat step 2.

8. Once you have reached the permanent area, your Morkie will be potty trained and will understand that the only designated area for going to the bathroom in the house is in the litter box.

Suggestions:

- Doggy litter is preferable to use instead of kitty litter, as puppies may try to eat the kitty litter. Doggy litter looks more like rabbit filler or pellets, which will turn to sawdust when wet. Doggy litter is biodegradable.

- Once you decide on a certain brand of litter, continue using that brand to avoid confusing your puppy. If you do decide to switch to kitty litter when your Morkie is older, begin by mixing the new kitty litter gradually into the doggy litter.

- The litter box is not meant to replace going to the bathroom outside, it is to be used as backup for when you can't take your Morkie outside. You should still set aside time to daily take your Morkie outside to play and walk.

- It is easier to litter box train your Morkie when it is still very young. It is possible with older pups, but it will be more of a challenge.

- Try placing the litter box close to the outside door, which your Morkie probably already associates with going to the bathroom.
- Tiled areas are easiest for clean up, but if only carpeted areas are available, put plastic or newspaper underneath the litter box.

Before bringing home your Morkie, make sure you purchase a litter box designed for smaller dogs at your local pet supply store. Depending on the size of your Morkie when fully grown a cat litter box might be sufficient.

If your Morkie is male, try to find a litter box with a higher side, in case he decides to lift his leg when peeing. Make sure the entrance to the litter box is low enough to allow easy access for your Morkie's small legs.

Just as with potty training your Morkie outside, you will want to follow the schedule found in this chapter for when to take your Morkie to the litter box.

Watch carefully for any signs that it needs to go to the bathroom, such as circling, squatting or smelling intensely in a certain area. When you see this type of activity, quickly but carefully pick up your Morkie and take it to its box, then say your command to go the bathroom.

Praise your pup every time it goes to the bathroom near to or in the litter box. Remember, it wants to please you, so it will repeat this behavior.

Dogs do not have the behavioral instincts that cats have to use a litter box. Litter box training is possible with extra effort and patience on your part. As with everything in life, you only get out of it what you put into it. It will take time and energy to litter box train your Morkie, but it will give you peace of mind in the future.

As with all types of potty training, accidents will happen, so be prepared to clean up and have lots of patience with your baby Morkie.

How to potty train an older Morkie

If you have adopted a rescue dog from your local shelter, it most likely hasn't been properly trained and that's why it was dropped off at the shelter. If your Morkie was potty trained but has spent some time in a shelter, it will most likely need a refresher course on potty training, as it didn't get regular walks at the shelter.

You can teach an old dog new tricks--with a bit of time and patience.

The key to successfully potty training an older Morkie is to begin the minute we bring it home. It is recommended to use the crate training method for the first week and then begin to combine crate training with den training, by using the crate with the door open, slowly expanding the den space.

Step one:

Take the first week off to properly train your adult Morkie. Someone will need to take your adult dog out for walks or to the designated spot. The best person to do this is you, so your adult dog can begin to bond with you.

Step two:

Begin using the crate from day one. Crate training is a good solution for potty training your adult dog, since it won't like to spoil its sleeping and eating areas.

Make sure the crate is big enough for your Morkie to stand up and turn around in. If it is too big, your adult dog might decide that there is room to go to the bathroom in the corner. Keep the crate in a high-traffic part of the house, so your dog doesn't feel isolated and alone.

Make sure the crate is only used when necessary; give your new dog lots of playtime, exercise and obedience training outside of the crate.

If you don't think using a crate is humane, please understand that you won't have to use it for very long, (three or four days maximum) until your adult dog is potty trained.

Step three:

Give your adult Morkie at least six to eight bathroom breaks a day.

It will need to go to the bathroom when you wake up and before you go to bed, after meals, and after drinking water or playing. Once potty trained, it will normally only need to relieve itself four to five times a day.

Step four:

Generously praise and reward it when it relieves itself in the designated area.

Praise and rewards send a message to your dog's brain, telling it that this behavior is beneficial. It will repeat the behavior to be rewarded again, and after time it will become part of the routine.

Make sure the praise and rewards come right after the action. You want your dog to clearly understand that eliminating in the designated spot is the best thing in the world for you. Don't wait to give the treat later, as your dog will not be able to associate the treat with relieving itself.

After your dog goes to the bathroom, give it some playtime as a reward. If you only take it outside for the bathroom, it will quickly learn to linger before going the bathroom, just to prolong the time outside with you.

Step five:

Never punish your dog for accidents that you did not actually see happen. If you catch it in the act, startle it midstream with a clap, then quickly take it to the designated spot so it can finish the job.

Clean up thoroughly so it isn't enticed to return the same spot by the enzymes left by the urine or poop.

Leave the soiled towels near the designated spot; the scent will reinforce your dog to relieve itself at that spot.

When cleaning up, stay away from ammonia-based cleaners, as they smell like urine to your dog and it will want to go pee again on the same spot.

Bottom line: Crate training is extremely effective for potty training an older dog and it will only be temporary. Remember to generously praise and reward your Morkie every time it goes in the designated spot. At all costs, avoid punishing your Morkie for bad behavior; this will make potty training almost impossible.

Overview:

The main ingredients needed for potty training your Morkie are patience and a huge dose of love, plus following all of the instructions in this chapter. Potty training should not take longer than a week, but there might still be an occasional accident, as your dog learns to control its bodily functions.

Have you ever heard the expression "don't cry over spilled milk"? It means there is no need to make a big deal about something that has happened; it happened and you can't change it. This should be your philosophy while potty training your Morkie. There will be accidents, so don't make a big deal about it.

If your Morkie has an accident, most likely it was your fault for not paying attention to the signals that it needed to go to the bathroom. The only thing to be done is to clean up the mess and get on with your life.

Potty training will take only a few days out of your busy life, the result being a well-behaved dog that you can let roam around your house worry-free. Take time to apply the suggestions found in this chapter, and in no time you'll have the best-behaved dog on the block.

CHAPTER FIVE
Obedience training

"Morkies are some of the cutest puppies in the world. Sometimes owners tend to let them get by with bad behavior because "they are so cute", but they do still need to be trained and socialized just like their bigger cousins."

Pam Peterson
www.royalkennels.com

Morkies are considered to be one of the easiest dogs to train because they are extremely intelligent, good tempered and are eager to please their owners. But the sad reality is that most Morkies are spoiled rotten brats. Why?

How to train

The problem with all of these spoiled rotten Morkies lies with their owners. They did not take the time and effort to properly train them.

Parents have to take the time to teach their children good behavior; if they don't, the children will turn into spoiled rotten little brats. A young child's bad behavior, if not corrected, will become part of his or her personality. These personality traits become deep-rooted and almost impossible to correct later on in life.

The same thing can occur with Morkies. They can either be molded positively or negatively. Successful obedience training depends exclusively on how much energy and time you are willing to invest in your Morkie's obedience training.

Children who are little brats are a direct reflection of their parents. Our normal reaction (right or wrong) when we see a disobedient child throwing a tantrum is to blame the mother and think to ourselves, "Why doesn't she teach her child to behave better?" The same applies to your Morkie; its behavior is a direct reflection on you.

One of the main reasons that Morkie owners don't properly train their puppies is due to their itsy-bitsy size. They look so innocent and cute. Most Morkie owners don't have the heart to discipline them. But that adorable looking puppy can turn into a badly-behaved brat in matter of weeks.

Many Morkie owners consider their puppies to be much less threatening than bigger dogs. But the truth of the matter is it doesn't matter how big your dog is: big or small, all dogs can deliver bites that can seriously endanger a human. Also, all dogs can escape and run into traffic.

As with everything in life, the results depend entirely on how much effort you are willing to invest. You need to realize from the minute you pick your puppy up and bring it home that you will need to invest serious time and energy in training this puppy.

Training will include potty training, obedience training, leash training and teaching your puppy to interact with other people and dogs. Training also provides an ideal situation for bonding with your Morkie.

By taking the time to train your Morkie, you are ensuring its own safety and the safety of those around it.

Four basic commands to teach your Morkie

Here are some of the most basic commands that you will need to teach your Morkie. These basic commands will be the foundation for further training in the future and will prevent behavioral issues later on in life.

All of these commands are very simple to teach and provide an excellent opportunity to bond with your puppy.

Sit

This is one of the easiest and most important commands to teach your Morkie.

1. Show your Morkie a treat and hold it up to its nose.
2. Slowly, move your hand up above its head. It will follow the treat with its head and sit down.
3. Once it is sitting, say the key word "sit," then give it the treat and generously praise it.
4. Repeat steps 1 through 3 a few times during the day, until your Morkie has mastered it. Then begin to ask your dog to sit before going for walks, mealtime and any other situation. Make sure you always praise your puppy for sitting when asked.

Come

This is another common command that you will frequently use to call your Morkie, to keep it from going too far from you or to avoid unfortunate accidents.

1. Put your dog's leash and collar on.
2. Get down to its level and say, "come." While saying "come," gently pull on the leash to bring your dog towards you.
3. When it comes to you, give it a treat and generously praise it.
4. Repeat steps 1 through 3 until your dog has mastered the command. Then begin to practice without the leash, in a safe enclosed area where your Morkie can't run away.

Down

This is one of the trickiest commands to teach your Morkie, but you will be so grateful if you both master it, as it will save you much heartache later on. It is considered to be difficult because the dog by natural instinct considers it to be an act of submissiveness. Try to keep a relaxed attitude with your Morkie while teaching it this command.

1. Choose your pup's favorite treat and hold it inside of your closed fist. Make sure it has a strong smell.
2. Hold your fist up to your Morkie's nose and let it have a sniff. Then move your hand to the floor. Your dog's head will follow your hand to the floor.
3. Once its head is close to the floor, slide your hand along the ground in the area in front of it. This will encourage it to be in a semi-sitting laying position, with all four legs on the floor.
4. Once your dog is in that position, say "Down," give the treat and generously praise it.
5. Repeat steps 1 through 4 until your dog has mastered the command. Repeat every day. If your puppy tries to jump forward or sit up, say "No" and take your hand away. Never push it into the down position. Generously encourage every step or movement your puppy makes towards going into the down position, as it is re-programming its natural instincts.

Stay

This is an excellent command to teach your Morkie, but don't even begin to teach it to your puppy until it has mastered the "Sit" command. This exercise will be teaching your Morkie self-control. It is challenging for energetic Morkies, but remember that Rome wasn't built in a day either.

1. Tell your dog to "Sit".
2. Open your hand and make a stop sign with the palm of your hand and say, "Stay".
3. Take a few steps backwards. If your puppy stays in the same place, reward it with a treat and generous praise.

4. Each time you do steps 1 through 3, gradually increase the distance between you and your Morkie before you give it the treat.

5. Always give your puppy a treat for staying still, even if it only stayed still for a matter of seconds.

There are many other commands that you can teach your Morkie. As Morkies are extremely intelligent, you will find training to be a relatively easy task.

Should I take my Morkie to obedience classes?

If you have adopted a rescue dog or an older Morkie, it is highly recommended to take your Morkie to obedience classes, as it may be a little more stubborn at learning new tasks. Puppies can be like children in the sense that they lack coordination and can be easily distracted, but with a little orientation they can learn positive behavior.

Many dog owners recommend taking your dog to obedience school every two to three years. This will reinforce good behavior that might have gotten rusty over the years.

The sole purpose of obedience school is to help orient YOU in training your dog. Your dog will not have a miraculous transformation from just attending obedience school. The key is practicing everything that you both just learned at each obedience school class when you are at home. Practice and daily repetition of things learned will lead to a well-behaved and well-trained dog.

Photo Courtesy of
Rose Weaver

Obedience school will only reinforce the positive training that you are giving your Morkie at home and train you to be a more effective teacher.

Here are some suggestions to take into consideration before you take your Morkie to an obedience school.

• Make sure your Morkie's vaccinations are up to date and it doesn't have any other potential health issues. You don't want to expose your Morkie to diseases or put the other dogs at risk.

• Typically, obedience classes for dogs will accept dogs that are older than 6 months. If you want to enroll your puppy in classes before it is 6 months old, you can enroll it in puppy kindergarten classes that will teach it how to socialize with other dogs and a few basic commands.

- Make sure the instructor only uses humane methods for training dogs. Avoid institutions that punish dogs by hitting, scaring, yelling or using electric shocks for bad behavior. You want to look for training that will overlook bad behavior and reward good behavior.
- Ask where the trainer was certified to train dogs. You are paying for the classes, so make sure that the teacher didn't learn everything he or she knows online. A certified trainer has met the requirements of the International Association of Canine Professionals (IACP) or Certification Council for Pet Dog Trainers (CCPDT) and has already completed a significant number of hours training dogs.
- Ask to sit in on a class just to observe before signing your puppy up for the obedience class. This way, you can observe how the trainer treats the dogs and their owners. If the owners are treated with respect and care, the dogs will be too.

Teach with love, not fear

Many of us grew up in families that had dogs and we observed our parents training them. Love and patience may not have been the main ingredients used in training the dogs. The days of punishing our dogs for things they are incapable of understanding are over. Studies have shown that the best way to train a dog is by using positive reinforcement.

How can you use positive reinforcement to train your Morkie?

Dogs live in the present and not the past or future, so the best time to reward good behavior is when it happens. The dog needs to associate the good behavior with being rewarded. Rewards can be praise or treats, which it can receive every time it does something that pleases you.

✔ *Do praise and reward your Morkie immediately after it does the desired behavior.*

Make training sessions short and sweet. Your Morkie might be extremely intelligent but it has a short attention span, and even more so if it is still a puppy. The goal of each training session should be to leave the class on a positive note, leaving it wanting more.

✔ *Do make all training sessions short and sweet.*

Treats are treats, and they are meant to be something special. When starting obedience training, you will be giving your Morkie a lot of treats to motivate your pup to learn the positive new behavior.

Once it begins to master the new behavior or tasks, you will need to slowly phase out the treats and replace them with praise. When your puppy is growing it has a faster metabolism, so the extra calories are not a big deal, but as it gets older it means extra weight. If you must give treats to an older dog, reduce its portion for daily meals.

✔   *Do phase out treats and rewards as your Morkie begins to master the new tasks and replace them with praise and affection.*

Avoid making the training sessions overly complicated by using long key words such as "Stay here!" Simplify it by saying just "Stay!"

Dogs respond better to one-syllable key words and will be able to re-member them more easily. Be specific and simple when teaching your dog. Making the commands and instructions too complicated will just stress your dog out, making it dislike training time.

✘   *Don't make training sessions overly complicated.*

Inconsistency is your worst enemy in obedience training your Morkie. Morkies thrive on having a well-established routine. If you tell it today that it cannot sit on the couch when you allowed it to yesterday, this will just confuse your Morkie and make training more tedious.

Make sure everyone that lives under your roof is on the same page for training your Morkie. Otherwise it will be at its wits' end trying to fig-ure out what is allowed with whom and when.

✔   *Do be consistent in training your Morkie.*

Don't create a spoiled rotten puppy. Bad behavior needs to be cor-rected. When your Morkie acts up and does something inappropriate, don't just let it continue. Tell it "No" and redirect its attention to some-thing more productive.

✘   *Don't allow your Morkie to get away with bad behavior.*

A word about physical correction or punishment

Study after study has proven that physical punishment or correction is ineffective in training an animal. Why?

Imagine trying to do something while being yelled and screamed at or receiving painful electric shocks or being physically hit or kicked. Would you be able to learn something new under this type of stress? Of course not! You would be scared, nervous and very stressed out.

Most of us mentally shut down when we are being yelled at. We try to back away from the situation.

That is exactly how your Morkie feels when it is punished; it has no idea why you are mad or what it did wrong. Put yourself in your dog's paws. How would you like to be treated?

- Fear inhibits learning.
- Fear inhibits listening.
- Fear inhibits trust.

Never ever use physical punishment to correct your dog's bad behavior.

Say no to barking

Your Morkie comes from a line of barkers; both the Maltese and Yorkie are well-known for barking. Your Morkie has inherited the same love for barking that its parents had.

Barking is a habit that begins to form as your Morkie ages. Your Morkie most likely will be very quiet as a puppy and even as a young adult, but when it is about two to three years old, expect the barking to begin.

When your Morkie starts barking, you will need to discover the underlying cause behind it. Your Morkie will use barking as a way of communicating with you. If you are unable to determine the reason behind the barking, it will be almost impossible to stop.

Let's consider some reasons why your Morkie might be barking.

- **Fear:** Maybe there was a noise or a something out of place and it is frightened. Normally, this will be a fairly loud bark, because it is alarmed. This can happen in any location, not just your house.
- **Boredom:** Morkie dogs are very social and love human companionship. When they are left alone or ignored for long periods, they will quickly become lonely and bored. Barking is one of the less destructive ways they blow off their steam about being left alone. This type of barking can be extremely intense and very passionate on their part. This barking is a guaranteed way to get your neighbors to complain.
- **Stranger danger:** Morkie pups become very territorial as they get older, so when someone new approaches them, you, or your house, they will begin to bark. As the threat gets closer, the bark gets louder and louder. When your dog is barking for territorial reasons, it will be quite aggressive and protective.
- **Wanting attention:** Barking is your Morkie's way of communicating with you. It will bark to tell you it wants to go outside, eat, play or get a treat. You will need to use discernment for this type of bark, as it

will look at you, then the subject of what it wants to do (such as looking at the door to go outside).

How can you teach your Morkie not to bark?

All dogs bark but they can be taught that barking is unacceptable behavior. How can you teach your Morkie not be a barking terror?

As previously mentioned, boredom is one of the main reasons that your Morkie might start barking. Morkies are companion dogs, so they need to be around people. Morkies are known for forming a tight bond with their owners and thrive on attention.

If you find that your Morkie is constantly barking when it is left alone, it is trying to tell you that it is lonely and wants you to come back. How can you solve this problem?

Before trying to change your Morkie's behavior, try to change your daily routine, so it isn't at home alone too much. Maybe you can take it to work with you or arrange for a close friend to periodically drop in and visit during the day.

Reminders of what not to do:

Your reaction when your dog begins to bark can either discourage barking or encourage even more barking. Let's see how you can discourage this bad behavior.

Photo Courtesy of
Justin and Allana Robinson

Shouting at your dog to get it to stop barking is actually the worst thing you can do. It will get your Morkie even more excited as it thinks you have decided to join the barking, causing it to bark more. Never yell at your dog to tell it to stop barking. Instead speak calmly and tell it in a firm voice to be quiet.

All dogs have a natural instinct to bark when another dog barks at them. By yelling at your dog to stop barking, all you are doing is reinforcing the barking. The best thing to do is to stay quiet.

When your Morkie begins to bark, just ignore it until it stops barking. When it stops barking, then tell it to hush or be quiet. Wait for it to be quiet for twenty to thirty seconds and reward it for its good behavior. The key to training your Morkie not bark is to constantly reinforce this simple obedience exercise. As you are rewarding it for not barking, it will slowly begin to understand that barking is bad and that not barking means rewards.

Another way to stop your Morkie from barking is to distract it every time it starts to bark. When it begins a barking fit, call it over and ask it to do a command or trick for you. By interrupting your dog's barking, you reduce the chances of it forming a habit of barking.

If you notice that it seems to be barking when strangers come up to the house or you, then you will need to work with your dog so it feels comfortable around strangers. How can you do that?

The key lies in socializing your Morkie as much as possible. Invite friends and family over to your house and introduce them to your dog, making sure your Morkie feels safe and comfortable throughout the whole introduction process. If it begins to bark at someone, calm it down and help it see that the stranger isn't a threat to either of you.

Anti-barking collars: The American Society for Prevention of Animal Cruelty states the following: "Anti-barking collars are cruel and not effective." What is an anti-barking collar?

It is a collar that has a noise-sensitive device attached to it. When the device is activated by barking, it gives the dog a small electric shock; others spray a citrus spray.

These collars train dogs not to bark for any reason and can cause smaller dogs to become fearful and anxious. Also, intelligent dogs such as the Morkie quickly discover that they are only punished when wearing the collar.

Remember these four suggestions to train your Morkie not to bark:

1. Don't react
2. Don't shout
3. Distract
4. Socialize your dog as much as possible with other people

Barking up the wrong tree

None of us speak dog language and your dear little Morkie doesn't speak English. But you can learn to interpret what he is trying to tell you by barking; you just need to learn to listen to what the barking is telling you.

There are three qualities of dog barks that can help us distinguish the reason behind the bark: pitch, length and frequency.

- Low pitch: A lower pitched sound such as a growl indicates that a threat is nearby or the dog is upset and angry. Basically, it is saying "stay away from me or else".

- High pitch: A higher pitched sound like a sharp bark, whining, or a whimper means the opposite of a low pitch, meaning you are allowed to come closer and it is safe to approach. It is a welcome bark.

- Length: If the dog continues growling (low pitch), that typically means it really doesn't want you to come closer. The length of the sound means it is standing its ground and not backing down. If the growl is in short bursts, it means the dog is very concerned and fearful, but isn't sure if it can hold its ground or if it is totally necessary.

- Frequency: There will be barks, yelps or whining that are repeated again and again. The closer the sounds are together, the more excitement your Morkie wishes to express. If your Morkie just gives out an occasional bark, it is only slightly interested in something.

When your Morkie feels threatened or in danger, its barking will be combined with a low pitched growl. Here are some common interpretations for most barks.

- **2 to 4 barks in a row:** This is one of the most common forms of barking, which goes back to all dogs' roots from wolves, meaning, "Call the pack". This bark is telling you, his pack leader that something interesting is happening and he wants you to see it.

- **Barking slowly in a lower pitch but almost non-stop:** Your Morkie senses imminent danger. It means the stranger danger is very close and be prepared to defend yourself.

- **1 or 2 sharp high-pitched barks:** This is a typical greeting bark and once your Morkie realizes that the stranger is friendly, they will be greeted with this bark. It basically means "Hello there!"

- **A row of barks with a pause in between:** This is a sad bark, which means your Morkie feels very lonely and bored. It is his way of asking for some cuddle time and companionship.

- **'Harrruff' or stutter bark:** Normally, this bark is combined with playful body language, saying he is ready to play. His front legs will be flat on the ground and his rear held high in the air, he is ready to play.

As mentioned previously, you might discover that your Morkie was very quiet until he was an adult and suddenly becomes more vocal. Barking is a learned behavior, so the key is to nip it in the bud before it even begins. You will need to practice non-barking obedience training throughout your Morkies life.

Never ever allow your dog to bark uncontrollably.

Patience is a virtue

Obedience training can take a toll on you, as it is a long and tedious process that just doesn't happen overnight. The key to successfully training your Morkie is to be patient. You will need to realize that you are teaching your dog a whole new way of life.

Imagine that you are learning how to do ten different things at once and your teacher doesn't speak English. How would you feel? It sounds like an impossible feat. What qualities would you appreciate your teacher having? Most of us would agree that we would like them to have patience and understanding.

This comparison helps us put ourselves in our puppy's paws, as this is exactly how it probably feels. It really wants to please you but doesn't always understand what you are trying to tell it to do. So please be patient with your little Morkie.

Patience is needed because your Morkie will need time to learn and understand all of these new commands. What can help you to be patient during the training process?

You need to realize that your puppy has limits. Once you understand what those limits are you won't push too hard.

Younger dogs have a shorter attention span than older dogs and can be easily distracted. For this reason, it is advised to keep training sessions short and sweet.

Adult dogs can learn more complex tasks than younger dogs but can be stubborn at times. No matter how old your dog is, it can learn new tricks with repetition.

Morkies are eager to please their owners, but when they are puppies they tend to think everything is about playtime. Don't punish your Morkie for being a puppy; remember puppies will be puppies and that is one of the limitations at that age. You will need to do shorter training sessions with your Morkie puppy throughout the day until it is able to concentrate better.

If you have adopted a rescue dog that might have been mistreated, abused or physically punished in the past, it can be more difficult to train because it will have some serious trust issues. You will need to give it an extra-large dose of love and patience.

Your attitude towards training your puppy will play a very important part in how your Morkie will respond to you. If you are impatient or agitated, you will need to do shorter training sessions. Your dog can quickly pick up on your negative vibes and will imitate you. If you feel overwhelmed about how to train your Morkie, you can always enroll in an obedience class that will orient you better in how to train your dog.

Your dog and you both need to keep an open mind to learning new things and realize that training sessions provide a wonderful occasion for bonding with your puppy. By being patient and loving and constantly praising your little Morkie, you show your approval, making it to want to please you even more. Obedience training is a long process, so make it enjoyable and fun.

Sometimes to help your Morkie understand what you want, you will literally have to show it by doing it yourself. You might have to position the dog for what you want it do and reward it for just beginning to follow the command, even if it is only halfway done.

Training and rewards

Who doesn't enjoy a good meal or snack? We all do and your Morkie is no exception; it loves to eat. Treats are one of the best ways to motivate your Morkie to learn new tasks. It would be impossible to train any dog without yummy snacks as a reward for good behavior.

Many of the tasks you want to teach your puppy might be hard for it to comprehend what you want it to do. You will have to use a keyword or sound or even get down on your knees and show your puppy what to do. Even then, it still might not get it. But a treat makes everything easier for dogs to understand.

How to use treats in obedience training your Morkie

Small treats: All these treats and rewards are going to put stress on your Morkie's waistline. It is very easy to overdo it when giving your puppy treats while training. Try giving only small treats, or if possible, break the treats into pieces. If you found you gave out too many biscuits in one day, maybe you could give it less food for mealtime.

When to reward: Never ever reward bad behavior. By giving a treat you are reinforcing good behavior that you approve of. If your puppy goes into a hyperactive frenzy after doing the command, it will be best to wait to give the reward at another moment.

No bribes here: Reward training is temporary. It is used to motivate dogs in the beginning to learn a new habit and keyword. Over time, there will be more praise and attention for good behavior than treats. You will have to slowly phase the treats out; otherwise your dog will only behave when bribed by a treat.

*Photo Courtesy of
Katie Dee*

Reward each baby step: Many dog owners make the same mistake; they only reward their dog once it does the whole task perfectly before getting a treat. This only leads to frustration for you and your puppy. The key to successfully training your Morkie is to reward every baby step that it makes towards doing the task. Reward progress no matter how little it is.

Some days the progress might seem to be backwards, but we all have bad days. So give your little puppy some slack; it is trying its best to understand what you want. Over time, it will connect the dots and see that the treat is connected to doing a certain task.

Distractions: Puppies can easily be distracted. Make sure the training location you have chosen has no distractions. You want your Morkie to concentrate on you and the treat in your hand. Avoid areas where cars are driving by, children are playing nearby, or there are squirrels.

Something new: Keep your dog excited about the treats you are going to give it. Sometimes the treat you are going to give your puppy just isn't good enough for it to make such a big effort. For the more difficult tasks, choose your pup's favorite treats to motivate it to do the impossible.

Leash training

In a perfect world, dogs would be born knowing how to walk on a leash, but the reality is that you will have to patiently teach your puppy how to walk nicely on a leash. It needs to learn that it is incorrect to pull ahead or lag behind you.

The biggest challenge with training a Morkie to walk on a leash is to teach it to walk at your pace. Puppies are a bundle of energy and want to do and see everything at once. Plus they have one more set of legs than we have, which makes them move a little faster than we might want to.

Is it really necessary to use a leash and collar?

A leash is necessary because it helps keep your overly curious Morkie from getting into trouble, such as running head-on into traffic and getting hit by a car. Another reason why it is necessary to keep your Morkie on a leash is its keen sense of smell. If it were up to your Morkie, it would literally follow its nose and end up getting very lost.

Another reason you need to use a leash is that in most cities, it is required by law to walk your dog on a leash at all times. By using a leash you show those around you that you respect them and are a good neighbor. By having your dog on a leash, you can easily clean up after it when it goes to the bathroom on the sidewalk or somebody's yard.

If your dog is wandering about freely, it will most likely end up relieving itself out of sight and it will be left for someone else to pick up. Most cities have a hefty fine (up to $5000!) if you don't pick up your animal's excrement.

Collars carry your dog's identification, which will be handy if your Morkie gets lost. If there is no identification, somebody just might claim your dog as their own.

If your dog is found running at large it will be impounded, no questions asked. If your dog is impounded, the common fee is $50 for an impound fee and then an extra $15 per day. Plus, many shelters have extra fees added. These fees can be avoided by simply keeping your dog on a leash.

Leashes help keep your veterinary bills lower. This is because all dogs, including your Morkie, love to taste everything they smell and garbage is no exception. Also, free roaming dogs can get into poison ivy or oak, pesticides, or tick infested bushes, drink contaminated water, or walk through bushes with thorns or burrs.

Loose dogs can bite people. Dogs pick up on the stress around them and might accidently bite or scratch someone because they become frightened. If personal injury is caused, legal action could be taken against you and your dog. You might receive a hefty fine and your dog might be euthanized. Keeping your Morkie leashed helps keep your dog feeling safe and under control, and shows that you, the owner, are exercising reasonable precautions.

Walking your dog on a leash shows good etiquette. It shows you are a good neighbor and that you respect those around you. Not everyone loves your dog as much as you do. Some people might have severe allergies to dogs or phobias. Those suffering from phobias or panic attacks might react out of fear and injure your friendly Morkie if it runs up to greet them. Using a leash shows that you are in control of your dog and you respect those around you.

A leash is one of the most important items to have for your dog. It will be a protection for your dog, for those around you and for yourself.

How do you train your Morkie to use a leash?

If you follow these simple suggestions you will have your dog walking on a leash like a pro, in no time.

1. **Pick the best leash and collar for your Morkie:** Below, there is a brief introduction to the different types of leashes on the market. When choosing a collar for a new puppy, make sure it is lightweight and thin. You can always change the type of collar later on.

2. **Introduction:** Introduce your puppy to the leash and collar (or harness, if you are using one). Place the leash and collar or harness on it during playtimes. These should be very short periods in the beginning that gradually grow longer and longer. Eventually, the collar will stay on permanently. During these short periods of training your Morkie to like the leash, give it treats and praise it generously. It will begin to associate the leash and collar with food and fun time.

3. **Practice sessions:** Once your Morkie is accustomed to the leash and collar, walk it around the house with it on. Do not try and make it heel right away; the key is letting it understand the boundaries of the leash in the beginning. Walk a few steps with the leash, then stop and give your puppy a treat. Continue doing this until it begins to associate following your lead on the leash with getting delicious treats.

4. **Baby steps:** In the beginning, your puppy might try to wiggle its way out of the leash; just let it be, and once it figures out that the leash isn't going anywhere, continue walking. Try walking around the house, by the three-steps-and-a-treat method. Small steps will eventually lead to big steps, such as a walk around the block.

Types of collars and leashes

If you have ever looked at thve leash and collar selection at your lo-cal pet supply store, it can be very overwhelming. Here are some sim-ple suggestions to help you choose the best fit for your Morkie and you. If you have any doubts about the type of leash, ask your veterinary for recommendations.

Simple and basic leash and collar: This is the most common leash and collar and is a good fit for most dogs. When using this type of leash and collar, make sure you walk with your dog right beside or behind you; this will place you as the pack leader. This system is rec-ommended for Morkies.

Slip collar: This leash is used mostly for disobedient dogs, as it is a great way to correct bad behavior. The leash tightens around the neck when you pull or tug on it. It isn't recommended for smaller dogs, such as Morkies, as it could cause damage to their necks or restrict their breathing. It is mostly used for larger dogs.

Harness: This is a safe option for dogs that have a pushed-in face, such as Pugs and Pomeranians, or dogs with long, slender necks like Greyhounds. The harness will not restrict their breathing or damage their trachea and throat. This option is also recommended for Morkies.

Using a leash provides you with a silent way of communicating with your dog, by the energy you send through the leash. Without saying any-thing, you can tell it when to stop, walk, walk faster, etc. Never pull the leash or use excessive force.

When walking your dog, send a message by walking straight with your head held high as if you are your Morkie's pack leader; this energy will be sent down the leash to your Morkie.

Importance of visibility when walking your Morkie

Visibility means safety. At nighttime or early in the morning, it can be difficult for drivers to see you walking your dog. You might wear some sort of reflective clothing or a vest, and you can also purchase a safety harness that has reflective stickers on it for your dog. Also, many leash-es and collars have added illumination to protect your dog from acci-dents. You can even purchase reflective tape at your local hardware store and make your own reflective harness and leash for your Morkie, if you wish to save money.

CHAPTER SIX
How to care for your Morkie

"There is more happiness in giving than receiving" states a famous proverb. Properly grooming your Morkie will mean giving of your time, energy and maybe cash, but it will bring so much joy and happiness.

Wouldn't you love a spa day that gives you the full package: nails, massage, exfoliation, and then to top it off, getting your hair cut? You would feel like a new person by the end of the day. Your Morkie might not feel the same way as you do about going to get its hair done, but it can learn to love being groomed if you approach grooming correctly.

Taking care of your Morkie can bring both of you much happiness. Your Morkie is unable to fend for itself and will depend on you for all of its basic needs. You will have the honor of providing shelter, love, food, and all other necessities, including bathing and grooming.

Grooming basics

Your Morkie's parents, the Maltese and Yorkshire terrier, are both high-maintenance dogs because they require regular brushing and grooming. Your Morkie will require the same upkeep, as it has inherited the beautiful coat of its parents.

The type of hair your Morkie has will be the determining factor as to how often your Morkie will need to be groomed. It will be necessary to adapt your Morkie's grooming schedule to the dominant genes it has inherited from its parents. If the Maltese genes dominate, it will need a little extra grooming.

Here is a list of common hair types for Morkies:
1. Straight and thin: Morkies will have this hair type when the dominant gene is from the Maltese. This type of hair is not prone to knots or tangling, as the following types of fur are.

This type of hair is very elegant and beautiful but it requires quite a bit of upkeep. It is recommended to get this type of hair groomed and trimmed every six to eight weeks.

This hair type can easily be styled into hundreds of adorable haircuts, such as the puppy cut. It can also be grown long to look like a typical Maltese.

This type of fur has a very fine cotton-like texture that tends to mat quickly; it will need daily brushing to keep it in good condition.

2. Thick and silky: If your Morkie has this type of hair, it has inherited the dominant genes from the Yorkshire terrier. This type of hair is thick and silky and doesn't tend to mat as frequently.

Make sure you brush this type of hair at least twice a week to keep it looking neat and tidy. Brushing also helps to prevent tangles or knots from forming.

*Photo Courtesy of
Carla Kelican*

This hair type has body and sometimes it might have a light curl to it, making it easy to style into an endless list of haircuts that will make your Morkie the cutest dog on the block. It is recommended to get this type of fur trimmed and groomed every six to eight weeks.

Both fur types can grow long quickly, like the Maltese. If you decide to let the hair grow longer, it is recommended to get it trimmed and groomed every four weeks.

If your Morkie has curly, wiry or wavy fur, it is a sign of bad breeding practices. Most likely, it wasn't bred with a purebred Yorkshire terrier and a purebred Maltese. This is one of the hardest types of fur to maintain, as it is prone to matting and tangles. The wiry texture always looks messy, even after just being trimmed and groomed. The best hair cut for this hair type is to keep it as short as possible.

The options for styling your Morkie's hair are endless but here is a small list of some of the more popular haircuts. You can try a new one at each grooming until you find the perfect one that allows your Morkie's personality to shine through.

- **Miami Beach Cut:** This is one of the most popular styles for all dogs and Morkies are no exception. The face, tail and feet are shaved, leaving a pom-pom shape at the base of the feet, top of the head and the end of the tail. Then the rest of the body is trimmed.

- **Town and Country Cut:** This cut is recommended for all types of Morkie pups. This is a great haircut for your stylish Morkie who loves to play outside. This cut involves shaving the belly, face and legs. The rest of the hair is trimmed and can be left the length you desire and kept up by daily brushing.

- **Kennel Cut:** Also called the military cut. This type of haircut is recommended for all types of Morkies. The ears are trimmed and brushed out. Using scissors, the groomer will contour the hair on the body; the feet, face and tail are shaved, leaving a pom-pom at the end of the tail.

- **Lamb Cut:** This cut looks adorable on Morkies. The whole body is trimmed to the same length except for the tail, which has a pom-pom at the end. Gorgeous!

- **Puppy Cut:** This the most popular cut for Morkies. The fur on the whole body is cut close to the body and the hair on the head is brushed and made into a ponytail.

- **Continental Cut:** The fur on the entire body is contoured closely to the body; except the feet, which have pom-poms at the bottoms. So cute you will have everyone ooh-ing and ah-ing as your Morkie walks down the street.

As you can see, there are a lot of options for haircuts for your Morkie. If you decide to trim and groom your Morkie yourself, it is highly recommended to get the first haircut done by a professional groomer, so you can just follow the shape of the haircut the next time.

Start early

Whether you decide to get your Morkie groomed professionally or DIY, your Morkie will need to be trained to be groomed and to have daily brushing sessions. If you don't train it to be groomed and brushed when it is young, these sessions can turn into a constant headache for you.

As with children, the sooner they learn a new habit, the faster it becomes a routine and a well-established behavior. The sooner you introduce your Morkie to daily brushing sessions or to the groomer, the better the sessions will be in the long run.

Your Morkie will need to groomed and brushed for its whole life, so it is of utmost importance that it isn't terrified of the groomer or of the brush. The secret to avoiding that is to make sure its first introduction to the groomer and the brush doesn't traumatize it for life.

From the very first day that you bring your Morkie home, you will need to introduce it to the brush. Let your puppy smell and touch it, but under no circumstances allow it to chew or play with the brush. That will teach bad behavior. You want to teach it that the brush does not represent playtime but brushing time.

Once you have introduced the brush and your puppy realizes that it is not a threat, begin to lightly brush. Praise your puppy the whole time, using a soft voice and giving it some of its favorite treats the whole time. Only brush for a minute or two, and then play with your Morkie a bit. Repeat this process as much as possible the first few days after bringing it home, each time generously praising and rewarding it with treats, and it will begin to associate the brush with yummy treats. Over time, brushing will become normal and just a part of the daily schedule.

When grooming and brushing your Morkie, make sure all interactions are positive for your Morkie and yourself. If you find you dread grooming and brushing your pup, take it as a warning sign not to brush it right at that moment.

Your Morkie can pick up on your negative vibe and will not enjoy the grooming session either. Wait till you are in the right frame of mind before brushing your Morkie; this will help to make grooming sessions positive. You might need to give yourself a treat too, to motivate yourself to brush your pup. Maybe give yourself a dollar every time you successfully brush your Morkie.

When training your Morkie to be groomed and brushed, remember that longer training sessions are not necessarily better; keep them short and sweet. If you notice your Morkie is reluctant to let you brush it, it is sign you are pushing it, so you will need to cut the sessions shorter. You might want to use your Morkie's favorite treats to bribe it to enjoy grooming sessions.

Make sure you are prepared to begin brushing your Morkie from the first day you bring it home and for the rest of its life.

If you don't train your Morkie to like being brushed and groomed, you will be stressed out and the session will be uncomfortable for both of you, causing your Morkie to be traumatized and hate being groomed. Your Morkie might even resort to using force to show you how much it dislikes being groomed by biting, scratching, or growling at you, which will lead to you feeling traumatized every time you need to groom your little pooch.

So take the time to train your Morkie to enjoy being groomed and brushed; teach it that grooming is fun and it is a bonding time with you that includes delicious snacks.

Bathing

It is recommended to bathe your Morkie every three to four weeks. If you bathe your dog more often than every three to four weeks, you can cause its skin to dry out by washing away the natural oils. On the other hand, not washing your Morkie enough can cause its fur to become greasy and tangled. Blocked skin pores can cause your Morkie to have an unpleasant odor.

When bathing your Morkie, the key is using a good quality dog shampoo and conditioner designed for straight-haired dogs.

How to give your Morkie a bath

1. **Get yourself ready.** Make sure you are wearing clothes that you don't mind getting wet, dirty and hairy. Gather all the supplies that you will need during the bath, as you don't want to have to run and get something, leaving a wet and soapy puppy alone in the room.

   Make sure you have on hand: shampoo, conditioner, brush, and mineral oil for eyes, cotton balls or gauze for the ears, two big towels, and most important, lots and lots of treats. If you don't have a detachable showerhead, make sure you have a large container to help rinse your Morkie off.

2. **Fill up the tub or sink with warm water.** This is one of the common mistakes new dog owners make. They put the dog in an empty

sink and then begin to fill it up with water. This will only lead to your puppy becoming bored and the bath will be a bad experience.

3. **Get your Morkie ready**. Make sure your puppy's nails have been trimmed first, to avoid accidents. Bring it into the bathroom and shut the door behind you. This will prevent your wet, soapy dog from running around your whole house. Once in the room, praise it generously and give it some treats.

Try to make it feel really comfortable in the bathroom before you put it in the tub or sink. If your puppy lets you, put a cotton ball in each ear to prevent water from going in; just don't forget to remove them when finished. If your Morkie has sensitive eyes, you can put a drop of mineral oil in each eye, to prevent the shampoo from irritating its eyes.

Photo Courtesy of Ivana Cox

4. **Start washing.** Make sure you read the directions on the shampoo bottle so you use the right amount of shampoo. Gently place your pup in the tub or sink, making sure the water isn't too hot or too cold. Wet your dog's coat with water before you begin shampooing. Begin shampooing at the shoulders, then move on from there. Be very careful around the mouth and ears. Rinse out all the shampoo, using your fingers to assure all of shampoo has been removed, as residue could irritate the skin.

5. Detangle that fur. Once you have finished shampooing, you can apply the conditioner. Carefully follow the directions, as some conditioners require sitting for a couple of minutes to soak in. Rinse thoroughly.

6. Clean ears. While the conditioner is soaking into the coat is a good time to wipe your pup's ears clean with the gauze or cotton balls.

7. Towel dry: Take your puppy out of the sink or tub and quickly wrap it in a towel and try to dry it as quickly as possible. Avoid letting it shake itself until it is almost dry. Brush your dog's coat before you let it go out of the room, as baths help all the loose hair fall out. Beware, once you let your dog out of the room, it will go crazy and run everywhere. It is the doggy way to relieve stress.

Drying

As mentioned previously, you can towel dry your Morkie during the warm summer months, but it is even better to dry your Morkie with a hair dryer on low. Using a hair dryer also helps avoid tangling and knotting. When using a hair dryer, avoid pointing it directly at your Morkie's face, so you don't frighten it.

Brush the hair while you use the hair dryer. Brush the hair up towards the head, allowing the warm air to dry the roots. Be careful not to burn your little Morkie's skin--keep the hairdryer at least a foot length away from the skin and only use the lowest heat setting. Using a hair dryer will help remove excess hair that will form tangles and mats.

An excellent suggestion to avoid spending a long time brushing after the bath is to brush out dead hair before you give the bath. If not brushed out beforehand, it will most likely begin to fall out after the bath and be left all over your house, meaning more cleaning up for you.

Make sure your Morkie is completely dry before letting it outside, as it is prone to getting sick or catching a cold. Also, the whole bath and drying process can stress your little pup out and lower its immune system, so allow it take it easy the first twenty-four hours after having a bath.

Brushing

No matter what type of fur your Morkie has, you will need to brush it daily or at least every three days. Try using a pin brush or a slicker brush as these types of brushes are designed for Yorkshire terrier and Maltese hair types.

How to brush your Morkie's hair:

1. Gently sweep the brush through your Morkie's hair, being careful not to use too much force or pull at the hair.

2. As you are brushing, you will be removing the excess hair. Make sure you take out the hair that is collected by the brush occasionally. Leaving it there will make the brush less effective.

3. One of the best things to help detangle your Morkie's hair is a detangling spray that you can purchase at your local pet supply store. The spray will help remove tangles and prevent them from forming in the first place.

Photo Courtesy of Nancy Oz

How to remove a mat:

a. This can be a challenge as it will be uncomfortable for your little puppy and for you too, as you try to avoid hurting it. A little mat or tangle can quickly grow into a big mess in a matter of hours, so the key is nipping it in the bud before it grows bigger. Remember, a little discomfort in the beginning is better than much more pain in the future.

b. When you discover a mat or a tangle, spray it with the detangling spray, which will help loosen up the hair, making it easier to detangle. Then you will want to use a brush designed for mats or tangles and gently begin to tease the edge of the mat. It will take a little bit of time, but you will find that most mats or tangles can easily be removed by brushing.

c. You might encounter a stubborn mat that is just too big to brush out, so what can you do? When that happens, there is only one option: you will have to cut it out. Be very careful to cut out just the mat, as you don't want to snip your puppy's skin. Use your fingers to shield your Morkie's skin from the sharp scissors.

d. If you want to avoid cutting a piece of your Morkie's hair off you can always cut the mat in half, or if it is really big, cut it into three parts and begin to brush the mat out, little by little. By doing this, you will avoid having gaps of fur missing in your Morkie's coat.

If you notice that your Morkie is having a difficult time sitting still during a brushing session, the best thing to do would be to put the session on hold and have a serious playtime, so it can burn off its excess energy. Once it is all tuckered out, it will be ready for another brushing session. Forcing your Morkie to be brushed when it doesn't want to be will only cause you frustration and irritate your puppy.

Ears

Morkies are prone to ear infections, as are their parents, the Yorkshire terrier and the Maltese. For this reason, you will need to check your Morkie's ears weekly for signs of infection.

Just as you can get a buildup of wax in your ears, so can your Morkie. The adorable droopy ears your Morkie inherited from its parents make the situation a little more problematic and can lead to bad infections.

All dogs are very sensitive about having their ears touched and your Morkie is no exception, as it is a ticklish area. The key is to begin touching its ears early, as it will get used to being touched there, thus making it less sensitive or ticklish. Daily touch the ears by softly massaging them, while looking inside of the ears for infections. As you touch the ears, talk to your puppy and tell it what a good dog it is. Because it will be used to its ears being touched, it will not resist or try to bite when they are touched later in life.

If you have adopted an older Morkie pup that dislikes its ears being touched, try touching its ears each day. Each time, praise it generously and give it a treat. Try to touch the ears a little bit longer every day, until your dog is used to its ears being touched.

How to clean your Morkie's ears

1. Flip your Morkie's ears up and look for any signs of infection, such as pus or a sweet smell. Remove any debris that might be in the ears, such as grass, seeds or dirt. Then using a small damp cloth, gently wipe the ears clean and use a cotton swab to remove any ear wax.

2. Check to see if there are any signs of damage to the ears, such as small cuts or scratches that your Morkie might have made by accident when scratching its ears. If you find a small cut, just wipe it clean and let it heal naturally, but keep a close eye on it to make sure no infections develop.

3. If you notice a strong odor coming from the ears, that is a sure-fire sign of an infection. You should take your Morkie to the vet as soon as possible. Also take it to the vet immediately if you notice swelling or heat from a certain spot in the ear.

4. Use tweezers to remove any long hairs that might be growing out of the ears, as these hairs could lead to a future infection if not removed.

Nails

Your Morkie's nails grow at the same speed your nails grow. But the frequency with which your Morkie's nails will need to be clipped will depend entirely on the type of activity your Morkie regularly does. For example, if you often take your Morkie for walks on paved streets instead of grass, its nails will wear down faster. A dog who is walked on grass more than pavement will need its nails clipped more often.

You can clip your Morkie's nails, or if you prefer, you can ask your Morkie's groomer to cut its nails.

How to cut your Morkie's nails:

You will need to invest in a pair of nail clippers designed for smaller dogs. Also make sure you have some cornstarch on hand.

a. Make sure your Morkie is all tuckered out before you begin to cut its nails, as it will be less likely to fight back.

b. Gently pick up one of its paws and hold it in your hand. Examine the nails closely and identify the nail bed. If you cut into the nail bed, it will bleed and hurt your little baby.

How can you identify the nail bed? It is easier to notice in lighter-colored Morkies and more difficult to do so with darker-colored Morkies. Look for a little pink in the nail and cut above it by two millimeters.

c. Following the instructions that came with your nail clippers, place the clipper on your dog's paw and begin clipping, avoiding getting too close to the nail bed. Most nail clippers will need to be held perpendicular as opposed to human nail clippers that are held diagonally.

d. Work as fast as you can and don't take offense if your Morkie tries to pull away from you. If it yelps or cries that means you cut too low and hit the nail bed. It will soon begin to bleed, so quickly place your Morkie's paw into cornstarch to stop the bleeding.

e. You might not be able to cut more than one paw in each nail cutting session (or maybe even one nail each time), but it is something, so don't feel bad. A few dogs are very laid back about getting their nails cut but most will protest and try to escape.

As mentioned previously, you will need to get your Morkie accustomed to having its paws touched from the very first day you bring it home. Get it used to you touching its nails and holding its paws. Even if you decide to let a professional groomer cut your Morkie's nails, you still need to get it used to its nails being touched.

Rule of thumb: There is no written rule that says that you have to cut your Morkie's nails in one sitting. You can cut one nail per day, if that is all your Morkie will allow you!

Pedicure time for your Morkie

Many Morkie owners love to pamper their puppies. They keep them well-groomed and clean cut and love to put a little baling on their nails. If you decide to paint your Morkie's nails with nail polish, here are some simple suggestions to keep in mind.

- Morkie pups are curious by nature and love to lick or taste things that are new to them. For this reason, it is not recommended to use human nail polish as it contains chemicals that can be toxic if consumed. Taking into consideration the size of your Morkie, the toxicity can be fatal. Only use nail polish that has been designed for dogs.

- Before you apply the doggy nail polish, check your Morkie's nails for any cracks or cuts. The nail polish and nail polish remover can hurt your dog's skin.

- After applying the nail polish, carefully watch your Morkie. If it is chewing at the nail polish, that means it will be ingested, which will lead to an upset stomach. Normally, when Morkies are chewing at their nails, it is a sign that they are stressed. Never sacrifice your puppy's health for cosmetic reasons.

Extra care for your Morkie's nails and paws

Your Morkie is an inside dog but it loves to go for brisk walks and play outside. But during the long cold winter months your Morkie's delicate little paws can begin to dry out, become chapped and even cracked from the bitter cold outside and dry air inside of your house. How can you protect those paws?

One practical way is to apply a very small amount of coconut oil to the paws, as this will prevent the nails and paws from cracking and becoming painfully chapped. Just try to use a very small amount, as it smells delicious and your Morkie will try to lick it off. Coconut oil isn't toxic for your pup but it is high in calories which it doesn't need.

Maybe you are thinking is it really necessary to cut my dog's nails? Yes, it is, because if you don't cut your dog's nails they can easily split, which will lead to infections. And going for a walk on cement with overgrown nails doesn't sound very comfortable, does it? Walking with long nails can hurt your Morkie and cause it to limp, which could lead to costly posture problems in the near future.

Do-It-Yourself Paw Wax

This is a very simple and cost-effective recipe for making Paw Wax for your Morkie. It contains ingredients that are non-toxic for your dog and will protect the paws from the harsh chemicals on the ground in the winter or the burning hot cement in the summer. (It also makes great gifts for other pet owners!)

INGREDIENTS:
- 3 ounces of beeswax
- 3 tablespoons coconut oil
- 3 tablespoons avocado oil
- 3 tablespoons calendula oil (if you can't find calendula oil replace with avocado or coconut oil)

INSTRUCTIONS:
1. Stovetop: Put all the ingredients into a pot and melt. Stir occasionally. Pour into a plastic or metal container, let cool 20 minutes and it is ready to use.

2. Microwave: Place all the ingredients in a glass bowl and melt. Stir occasionally. Pour into a plastic or metal container, let cool 20 minutes and it is ready to use.

Teeth

You may have heard that your dog's mouth is cleaner than your mouth. But the truth is your dog's mouth is not clean. All dogs can develop tartar and plaque build-up and to top it off, many dogs suffer from gingivitis.

Worrying about your dog's yellow teeth and bad breath are just the beginning. Your Morkie can suffer from many of the same dental problems as humans. If not caught in time, these dental problems can lead to infections that can cause liver, heart and kidney failure that can sometimes be fatal. All of these dental problems can be avoided by practicing simple dental care.

The good news about your Morkie's teeth is that they are not as prone to cavities as your teeth are. How can you take care of your Morkie's teeth and avoid dental disease?

How to brush your Morkie's teeth

1. **Pick the right moment.** The best time to brush your puppy's teeth is when it is relaxed and calm. The goal is to set up a daily routine for brushing the teeth, if possible. If it has a healthy mouth, you could brush its teeth three times a week. Pick a time when your dog is normally relaxed each day and stick to it.

2. **Have your tools on hand.** Make sure you have toothpaste designed for dogs; one of the most popular flavors is peanut butter. (Make sure to use dog toothpaste only, as the fluoride in human toothpaste is toxic to dogs!) Also, use a toothbrush with soft bristles designed for small dogs, or you can opt for the finger brush. Be sure to have a treat ready to give your puppy as a reward for good behavior. Have the toothpaste already on the toothbrush.

3. **Get in position.** You both need to be comfortable. Avoid standing above your pooch or forcefully holding it down, as this will make your Morkie feel threatened. Kneel down beside your Morkie or place it at your level, if you are unable to kneel down. Make sure it is in a sitting position and you are right at its level.

4. **Check the gums.** Using light pressure, rub your clean fingers along the gums. This gets your puppy prepared for the toothbrush while you check for any wounds or broken teeth.

5. **Brush.** Lift up the upper lip and hold the toothbrush at a 45-degree angle, touching where the gums and teeth meet. Move the toothbrush in a circular motion, removing any plaque or tartar that has

Photo Courtesy of Laura Zezima

formed. Focus on the back teeth, as that is where plaque tends to build up. Aim to brush for about two minutes maximum.

6.   **Reassure your pup.** The whole time you are brushing, talk to your puppy in a reassuring voice, praising it for being such a good dog. This will keep it relaxed and at ease.

7.   **Reward your pup**. Once you have finished brushing its teeth, now it is time to reward it with a favorite treat and some special playtime with you.

As with all types of obedience training, it is vital to begin teaching your dog new behavior as soon as possible. The longer you postpone starting to brush your dog's teeth, the harder it will be. As it gets older, it will become agitated and upset when you touch its mouth and you may be afraid of being bitten with your hand that near to its teeth.

The best time to start training your Morkie for dental hygiene is while it is still a puppy, as it will be more carefree and easygoing about you touching its teeth.

From the very first day you bring your Morkie home, start rubbing your fingers over its gums and teeth. Keep repeating this daily until you actually start brushing the teeth. This will help it become used to the idea of its mouth being touched and it won't be defensive in the future.

As you know, your Morkie is extremely curious about everything, so before actually applying the toothpaste for the first time, let it smell the paste first and taste it. Place a very small dab on your fingertip and let it lick it off. If you notice that your pooch isn't too keen on the flavor, switch to another.

Once it is used to you touching its teeth and gums and likes the toothpaste, now is the time to introduce the toothbrush. Let your puppy smell it and lick it. Start by brushing only two teeth at a time, letting it get comfortable with the whole procedure.

Be prepared to see a little bit of blood the first couple times that you brush the teeth. Don't panic; slight bleeding is normal. But if you notice heavy bleeding that continues long after brushing, it is sign that you have been too aggressive or a warning sign of gum disease. If it is the latter, your Morkie should see the vet as soon as possible.

One easy way to clean your Morkie's teeth is by giving it crunchy food to eat. It is common for soft food to get stuck in the teeth, leading to tooth decay. Crunchy food helps keep the teeth clean but it should never be used as a replacement for brushing your dog's teeth.

Warning signs that your Morkie might have dental problems

Please, look weekly in your dog's mouth. If you notice any of the following symptoms, take your Morkie to the vet as soon as possible.
- Bad breath (not dog breath but bad breath)
- A change in your dog's chewing or eating habits
- Pawing at the mouth or face
- Depressed, not wanting to eat or play
- Excessive drooling
- Missing teeth (after the teething period, of course)
- Discolored or broken teeth
- Red, swollen gums or bleeding gums
- Growths or bumps inside of the mouth
- A yellowish-brown tartar buildup near to the gum line

How does dental disease affect your Morkie and you?

The dental tartar or plaque that builds up on your dog's teeth is made up of about 80 percent bacteria. If not removed, it begins to damage your dog's teeth and gums, the bones beneath the gums and the ligaments that hold the teeth in place. Once this bacterium spreads to the blood stream it can get into the heart, lungs and kidneys, causing a serious infection.

Advanced dental disease can be extremely painful for your loveable little Morkie, but it can all be avoided by properly cleaning your puppy's teeth.

Advanced dental disease will be very painful to your pocket book as well.

How often should a certified veterinarian check my dog's teeth?

Your dog's teeth should be checked out every six months to a year at most. Your certified veterinarian can check them out when you take your dog in for its check-up each year or every six months. Normally it is included in the cost of a check-up, but just make sure when you phone to make the appointment that it is included. If it isn't, request to add it on, so the veterinarian will have enough time to do your Morkie's check-up.

By taking the time now to provide proper dental hygiene, you will save yourself from much heartache in the future. If you don't care for your puppy's teeth, you can look forward to costly vet visits for your dog the probability of your dog having to receive anesthesia to have its teeth cleaned from the excess tartar and plaque buildup.

Take the time to train your dog to let you brush its teeth and you will both have something to smile about in the future.

Strengthening your Morkie's teeth

At your local pet supply store, you can find a wide variety of chew toys that are specifically designed to strengthen all types of dogs' teeth and gums. Avoid choosing chew toys that are hard and brittle and might lead to a broken tooth, then an infected tooth.

Many new dog owners wonder whether to let their dog chew on bones or not. It is fine for your dog to chew under supervision, as chewing on bones helps ward off plaque and tartar build up and strengthens the teeth. (Never, ever give your dog cooked poultry bones, which can splinter and cause internal injuries.)

These suggestions are not meant to replace regular dental hygiene for your dog's teeth, they are meant to assist in promoting good dental health. Would you chew gum and use mouthwash but not brush your teeth? No, because you know the most effective way to clean your teeth is by using a toothbrush and toothpaste. The same goes for your Morkie: dry dog food, chew toys and bones are only extras in promoting good dental health, like mouthwash and chewing gum are for you.

Retained baby (primary) teeth

Small dogs such as Yorkshire terriers, Maltese and of course your Morkie will often not lose their baby teeth due to their small jaw. These teeth will need to be pulled out by a certified veterinarian, to allow the stronger adult teeth to grow in. Normally, these primary teeth are pulled out when your Morkie is being neutered or spayed.

If your puppy's baby teeth are not removed, it will cause over-crowding in a very small jaw, causing the new adult teeth to not grow in straight. Crooked and uneven teeth easily trap food, causing it major plaque buildup. As we have already learned, plaque and tartar buildup are the main cause of stinky breath, gum disease and dental disease.

Periodontal disease:

Periodontal disease is a canine disease that is caused from plaque buildup. 80 percent of dogs that suffer from this condition have it because of the negligence of their owners for not taking the time to provide proper dental hygiene. This painful disease can be prevented by regularly brushing your dog's teeth.

This disease can cause your Morkie to be the world's most miserable dog, as it will make one of life's simplest pleasures, eating, very painful. If not caught in time, the bacteria can spread to the heart, liver and lungs.

If you notice that your Morkie has bad breath, it could be a sign of periodontal disease. Second, if you notice that your Morkie is drooling excessively, it might be a sign of gum disease. The drooling might be caused from pain or the salivary glands may be inflamed from the bacteria in its mouth. If you notice any of these signs, call your veterinarian and make an appointment to have its mouth examined.

Anal glands

Anal glands (also called anal sacs) are two little pockets located directly on either side of your dog's anus, one at 4 o'clock and the other at 8 o'clock. The glands should empty out through a very tiny duct into the anus. Each sac is filled with sebaceous oil glands and sweat glands. When these substances are combined or released through the anus, it comes out as brown fluid with a dreadful odor.

When you are grooming your Morkie, you will need to check the anal glands. If you are having your Morkie professionally groomed, ask your groomer to empty the anal glands. At your Morkie's annual check-up, request to have the anal glands emptied and checked to see if they are impacted.

Small dogs such as Morkies are prone to anal gland disease, especially if they are a little overweight. Normally, when a dog poops, the fluid in the anal sacs is pushed out. Problems begin when the sacs are not completely emptied. The fluid left behind in the sacs becomes dry and thick, causing the opening to plug up and the gland to becoming impacted.

These are four common signs of an impacted anal gland:
- Bad smell coming from the rear end

- Scooting
- Constipation or pain when pooping or sitting
- Trying to lick or bite the rear end

Impacted anal glands are very easy to treat. By gently squeezing near the anus, you can empty the sacs. It is recommended to do this before giving your Morkie its bath every three weeks, as you will be able to wash away the stinky smell.

1. **Suit up:** Wear old clothes and if you find the smell unbearable, put a clothespin on your nose. You can wear disposable latex gloves, if desired.

2. **Get ready:** Fold up several paper towels to absorb the nasty substance.

3. **Position your dog:** Looking at your Morkie's rear-end, lift up its tail and with one hand have the paper towel as close to the anus as possible.

4. **Squeeze:** Use your thumb and forefinger to very gently squeeze at the 4 and 8 o'clock positions, just below the anus. Use the anus as the clock face. Make sure your face is out of the way, as it is common for the liquid to squirt out of there.

5. **Clean up:** Throw the paper towels away, and wash your Morkie's rear end. It preferably to empty the anal sacs just before bath time.

Note: If you squeeze the anal sac and no anal sac fluid comes out, your Morkie might have an impacted sac, which means it will need to see the veterinarian soon.

If you find your Morkie is often having impacted anal sacs, you might need to add more fiber to its diet. This will increase the size of its poop, which will put more pressure on the anal sacs and help to push out the extra fluid.

The anal sac fluid is basically lubricant for your puppy, to help its poop come out more smoothly.

When left untreated, impacted anal sacs can become infected. If you notice yellow fluid or blood oozing out of the sacs, take your Morkie to the veterinarian. Your vet will have to clean the sacs out, which will be very painful for your Morkie, and give it antibiotics for a few days.

If the infection is left untreated, it turns into an abscess full of pus which is extremely painful for your Morkie. This abscess could break open at any time. Your veterinarian will have to open the abscess and clean it out. The vet will prescribe antibiotics and anti-inflammatory medicine to help the swelling go down.

If your Morkie keeps having problems with impacted anal glands, your veterinarian might recommend surgically removing the anal sacs. It is a simple operation, but often has side effects such as fecal incontinence, where poop leaks out uncontrollably.

How can you prevent impacted anal sacs?
- Healthy diet, with plenty of fiber
- Lots of exercise
- Regular vet check-ups
- Healthy weight (overweight Morkies have more issues with impacted anal sacs)

What if my dog won't let me touch its rear end?

This is a common problem, as the anus area is a very sensitive area for dogs.

The best way for your dog to get used to being touched in this area is to begin to get it used to this from the very first day you bring it home. As puppies are more adaptable and flexible, this will prevent the area from becoming overly sensitive.

If you find you just don't have the stomach to clean out your dog's anal glands, you can ask the groomer or veterinarian to do it for you at a nominal fee.

Tearstains

Tearstains are common for Yorkshire terriers and Maltese; hence it is a problem for your Morkie. Smaller dogs tend to suffer from watery eyes and the tears leave the fur wet around your pup's eyes, causing them to be stained.

In very extreme cases, these tearstains can spread to your dog's mouth and paws. Tearstains will leave a reddish rusty color around the eyes. Tearstains can be caused by a number of different factors: minerals found in the drinking water, yeast infection, eye irritation, allergies, poor food quality or blocked tear ducts.

Drinking water:

Many Maltese show dogs are only given distilled or bottled water to drink. The tap water found in most North American cities is packed with hard minerals that can irritate your Morkie, resulting in watery eyes.

Another factor that many pet owners forget to consider is that the water in the water bowl is contaminated because the bowl hasn't been properly cleaned. Most of the time, we just refill the water bowl without thinking about it. If you pay attention, you will notice a slimy buildup on the surface of the bowl. This is biofilm, which is made up of different bacteria (both good and bad) that have bonded together.

Biofilm can make your Morkie sick and it also causes watery eyes, which lead to tearstains. Also, the biofilm can cause your pup to suffer from diarrhea and an upset stomach. The germs can also spread around your house, putting you and your family at risk for illness. The only way to prevent the biofilm from forming is wash your Morkie's water dish daily.

How to clean your Morkie's water and food dishes:
1. Wash dishes with hot soapy water daily.
2. Use a dishcloth that is designated solely for your dog's dishes.
3. If you have a dishwasher, put them through the cycle at least once a week to kill off any unwanted bacteria. This will disinfect the bowls.

How to disinfect your Morkie's dishes if you don't have a dishwasher:

Option 1: Make a mixture using one part water and one part bleach and place the previously washed dishes in the solution. Let sit in the solution for ten minutes, then rinse and dry.

Option 2: Make a paste using one part water, one part baking soda and one part salt; mix all ingredients together to form a thick paste. Rub the prepared paste all over the dishes to scrub them clean, let sit five minutes, then rinse clean and dry.

When choosing water and food dishes for your Morkie, try to purchase dishes made from stainless steel or ceramic. Plastic bowls might be cute with their bright colors but the dyes used in plastic can irritate your Morkie's eyes. Many Maltese and Yorkshire terrier owners have complained that their dogs had bright red tearstains, which were directly related to a bright red food or water dish. It's best to avoid using plastic food and water dishes for your Morkie.

Yeast infections

There is a slight chance that the tear stains are being caused by a yeast infection in your Morkie's eyes or mouth. Normally, when a dog has a yeast infection in those places, it is caused by harmless red yeast that can easily be eliminated by a round of antibiotics.

Some veterinarians don't consider tearstains to be a serious issue and will not prescribe antibiotics for your Morkie. If you are concerned about it, it is time to look for a new veterinarian that is willing to listen to your concerns and take proper care of your Morkie.

Eye irritation

Sometimes a small object such as an eyelash or a piece of fur that is touching your Morkie's eyeball causes the tearstains. The foreign object irritates the sensitive tissue around your dog's eye, causing it to cry. If you notice your Morkie is crying, take time to check its eyes for anything that might be irritating them.

Also, because your Morkie has longer hair, it is common for the hair to grow over its eyes. Take the time to regularly trim the fur around your Morkie's eyes to help prevent tears and watery eyes. Another reason to remove excess hair around your dog's eyes is because it is more likely to trap bacteria and yeast, which can cause eye irritation and infections.

How can you remove your Morkie's tearstains?

There are quite a few ways to remove the unsightly tearstains from under your Morkie's eyes. Following is a simple recipe that is used world-wide by many show dog owners to remove tearstains.

1. In a small container place 1 tablespoon of Milk of magnesia, 1 table-spoon of Hydrogen peroxide and 1 tablespoon of cornstarch. Mix everything together until a thick paste is formed, adding more starch as needed.

2. Carefully apply under your Morkie's eyes. Avoid getting the mixture into your dog's eyes. Apply using a fine comb or an eyelash brush; brush the mixture away from the eyes in a downward motion.

3. Leave the paste on for several hours or overnight. Remove the dry paste by using a damp cloth. Apply on a daily basis or until the tearstains fade.

If you prefer, you can purchase premade tearstain remover for dogs at your local pet supply store.

Here is a simple homemade solution that will change the pH level of your dog's tears: adding a teaspoon of organic apple cider vinegar into your dog's water daily may help keep the tearstains away.

Before you remove the tearstain, it is recommended to ask your veterinarian if there are any health conditions causing the tearstains. Many times, tearstains are caused by injury, infection, ingrown eyelashes or unknown objects embedded in the eye.

Tools needed for grooming

It can be overwhelming to choose the equipment needed to correctly groom your Morkie. Not everything on this list is necessary, especially if you take your Morkie to a professional groomer. Some of these items can be purchased over time, as you need them.

Equipment needed for grooming your Morkie

- **Bristle brush:** This type of brush will remove any loose hair, dirt or debris. At the same time, it will stimulate your dog's skin, improve circulation and add a shine to the coat. This brush is ideal to remove hair. The bristles can cause injury to your dog, so be careful.
- **Pin brush:** The bristles on this brush are more widely spaced than the ones on the bristle brush. Also, the tips of the bristles are covered with a rubber tip, making them gentler when brushing. Groomers normally use this brush after the bristle brush, to fluff up the dog's hair.
- **Slicker brush:** This brush has short wire bristles packed closely together on a rectangular surface. This is an ideal tool for removing mats and tangles in your Morkie's hair. Groomers use them to make the dog's coat look smooth and shiny.
- **Mat splitters:** The name explains the purpose of this brush. Mat splitters come in three different types: letter opener, safety razor style and a curved blade style. These tools are used to split the matted fur into smaller pieces without causing your puppy too much discomfort. This will make untangling the mat easier.
- **Combs:** Combs are extremely useful in removing mats as they can get down to the root of the mat or tangle and slowly loosen it up. Some combs have rotating teeth, which make removing the tangles much easier with no need to pull your pup's fur.
- **Flea comb:** Again, the name describes the purpose of this comb. It is designed for removing fleas from your dog's coat. The flea comb is very small so it can fit into the spaces that are hard to reach, such as behind the ears, armpits, etc.
- **Scissors:** It is recommended to invest in a pair of high quality scissors to trim around the eyes between grooming sessions or to remove a troublesome mat that just doesn't want to be brushed away.
- **Shampoo and conditioner:** Make sure they have been designed for dogs and for the type of fur your Morkie has. Follow the instructions on the bottle.

- **Wash cloths:** One for washing your dog and the other for covering your dog's eyes during rinsing.
- **Big towels:** Used for drying your puppy off after the bath
- **Sterile gauze pads:** Used for cleaning the earwax and any dirt found in the ear.
- **Tweezers:** Used to pluck out any hair growing out of the ears.
- **Leave-in conditioner:** To prevent mats and tangles, this can be sprayed into the fur after grooming. Follow the instructions on the bottle.
- **Toothbrush and toothpaste:** You can purchase a toothpaste and toothbrush designed for dogs at your local pet supply store. You might need to experiment with different flavored toothpastes until you find the one that your dog tolerates best.
- **Nail clippers:** These come in all shapes and sizes, but you will want to choose one that is designed for smaller dogs.
- **Paw wax:** This can be purchased at your local pet store; it is used to protect your puppy's paws when outside during the bitter cold winter months and the burning hot summer months.

Going to the groomer

Your Morkie descended from a line of breeds that require special care and attention. Both Yorkshire terriers and Maltese have long, silky hair. It is possible to groom your dog at home, but most Morkie owners opt to take their dog to a professional groomer.

First impressions

You want your Morkie to love the groomer, so you need its first impression at the groomer to be a positive one. Before taking your Morkie to any groomer, you need to make sure that they are highly recommended and are willing to groom a Morkie. Some groomers only accept old clients or a certain type of dog.

Once you have picked out a groomer that you are interested in using, set up an appointment with the new groomer a few days before the actual grooming. During the meet and greet, your groomer can meet your Morkie and play with it for a few minutes. To make the introduction even more positive, make sure the groomer gives it a treat. By the end of the meet and greet, your Morkie puppy will love the groomer.

While your Morkie is greeting the groomer, try to slip out of sight for a few minutes. This will help your puppy understand that you will come back and you're not abandoning it forever with this strange person.

The purpose of the meet and greet with the groomer is to help break the ice before the actual grooming date. When you return to the groomer, your puppy will associate the groomer with a positive memory so it will not be traumatic when you leave it there and the bathing starts.

When you make the appointment for the meet and greet, request a time when there are no other dogs on the premises. If there are other dogs roaming about, it might intimidate your tiny little Morkie and make stress it out.

Photo Courtesy of
Ashley Jenkins

When should your Morkie go to the groomer for the first time?

It recommended to take your dog to the groomer for the first time after it is four months or older. Before four months of age, puppies are still extremely hyper and unable to sit still for the time needed to cut their fur and bathe them. No reputable groomers in their right mind are likely to accept a puppy less than four months of age, as they know the chances of accidently snipping the puppy are greater.

Is it really necessary to groom your Morkie?

Before answering that question, think about your own hair. What would happen if you didn't regularly get your hair trimmed? You could get split ends that, if not taken care of in time, can sometimes split right up the shaft, causing the hair to fall out. And to top that off, split ends can cause your hair to tangle easily.

Now what about you're Morkie?

If you don't get its fur trimmed regularly the same thing will happen to your Morkie. It will quickly develop split ends that will cause increased shedding, because the hair follicles have been weakened. More shedding will translate into more work for you, as you will have to clean up the hair that is stuck all over your furniture, carpet and clothes.

Not grooming your Morkie correctly will also make it prone to mats upon more mats. When your dog has mats, it is extremely painful, as the skin underneath those mats becomes red and inflamed because the matted fur is pulling and tugging on the skin. If the mat is not removed in time, the inflamed skin can become infected.

Grooming your Morkie isn't a cosmetic procedure; it is an essential part of your dog's health. Plus it will save you hours each week cleaning up hair and cutting out mats.

What kind of haircut should your Morkie have?

A good groomer will look at your Morkie and tell you what kind of haircut is best suited for the type of fur your dog has. There are no standard cuts for a Morkie, but generally speaking, the shorter the haircut, the easier it is to maintain.

A common hair cut for Morkies is the puppy or lion cut, where all of the fur on the body is cut quite short but left longer on the head, feet and tail. It is adorable!

Before choosing a specific cut, be sure to ask your groomer these questions:

1. How can I maintain the cut daily?
2. How can I keep my pet looking in top shape?
3. When should it come back for a trim and a wash?

Is it really necessary to use a professional groomer?

Do you cut your own hair? Some people do, to save money, but nothing beats getting your hair cut by somebody who knows what they are doing. Home haircuts don't always turn out as you intend.

The same goes for paying a professional groomer. Grooming your dog involves a lot of skill, training and special equipment. You can groom your dog's hair by yourself but at the risk of giving it a ridiculous looking haircut. Also, your wiggly Morkie doesn't understand the danger posed by the sharp scissors, so you could easily injure your pet. The conclusion is, if you can afford it, grooming is best left to the professionals.

When making an appointment make sure that a bath, nail cutting and hair trimming are all included in the price.

Hints your Groomer wishes you knew:

These are some helpful hints to make your Morkie's spa day even more wonderful for it and the groomer. These ten tips will benefit the physical and emotional well-being of your Morkie and make your groomer's job more enjoyable.

1. **Prepare your dog:** From the day you bring your puppy home, get it used to being touched in sensitive or ticklish areas such as its feet, ears and armpits.

   It is every groomer's nightmare to have to cut a dog's nails when it is skittish and upset because it can't stand its paws being touched. Make sure your puppy is used to being touched. Your groomer doesn't want to put the muzzle on your puppy, but might have to if your puppy tries and bite every time it is touched.

2. **Start grooming as early as possible:** Puppies are more adaptable than older dogs. That is why groomers wish all puppy parents would start having their puppies groomed by four months of age. Also, the earlier you start, the less matted the hair can get.

   The older the dog is, the more traumatic the experience will be. Never fall into the trap of thinking that your puppy doesn't need to be groomed yet. The longer you put it off, the more your puppy and the groomer will suffer.

3. **Brush regularly**: Your puppy's hair is like your hair. If you don't brush your hair for a couple of days it will look messy and become knotty and matted. The same goes for your Morkie: the less you brush its fur, the harder those knots and mats will be to remove.

Also, brushing your puppy regularly helps it not to be overly sensitive in certain areas, since it is used to being touched. Thus, it will not be nervous and upset during grooming sessions.

As mentioned before, matting can be a serious problem, causing your Morkie's skin to become irritated. Also, these mats can become far more difficult to remove, and in those cases, your groomer will just shave off the fur.

4. **Please give clear instructions:** Groomers can't read your mind and they work with several dogs each day, so be clear and specific as to what you want done. If you want a certain haircut, please bring in a picture to show your groomer. If you just want the nails cut and a quick trim, please let the groomer know. Communication is the key to a positive experience for all three of you.

5. **Listen to your groomer's suggestions:** Groomers are professionally trained and will have a general idea of what kind of cut will look good on your dog and what will look horrible. If your groomer suggests something different than you wanted, listen to the suggestions and sincerely consider them.

6. **Keep calm and don't stay and watch:** When you drop off your puppy at the groomer, be calm and relaxed as your pet can pick up on your negative and positive vibes. If you are stressed about leaving your little munchkin at the groomer, chances are it will be stressed too, leading to an uncomfortable experience for both your dog and the groomer.

By the way, don't drop by to see if your pet is finished or just to watch. Your puppy will hear your voice and get excited, making grooming almost impossible.

7. **Wash away:** Many pet owners are afraid that if they bathe their dog too often it will dry out their dog's skin. This isn't a problem if you choose the correct shampoo. If you are unsure what type of shampoo to use, ask your groomer for a recommendation. Frequent washing makes your groomer's job easier and will help avoid future skin problems.

Exercise

All living creatures need to exercise, and your Morkie is no exception. Even though your Morkie is an indoor dog and will be spending the majority of its time inside your house, it still needs to get regular daily exercise outside, in the fresh air.

Regular daily exercise will help to keep your dog's blood flowing, muscles strong, and little heart pumping and keeps it in tip-top shape. Plus having regular daily exercise will allow your dog to sleep better and keep its weight in check (these benefits will apply to you, too!).

One of the best aspects of regular exercise for your Morkie is that it promotes good behavior. Studies have proven that when a dog receives enough exercise, behavioral issues almost disappear. Regular walks around the block help your Morkie blow off all the extra energy it has; otherwise, that energy would be used in a negative way, such as chewing your throw pillows to pieces.

Outside exercise

This is going to be your pup's favorite time of the day. Most Morkies love being outside and will do anything to stay outside for as long as possible. Just use caution when introducing your Morkie to other dogs if it hasn't received all of its vaccines yet, as it is still prone to infections and can make other dogs sick too.

Many people think small dogs such as Morkies don't need exercise, but no matter their size, dogs need exercise. They won't need as much exercise as a bigger dog or be able to run long distances, but they will need some form of daily activity, no matter their age.

Because Morkies are so small, they need to be protected from the extreme cold and hot outside weather. Following are some suggestions on how to protect your puppy from extreme climates.

Cold weather: Morkies can get chilled very fast. On colder days, make sure you put a sweater on your pup, to protect it from the bitter cold winds. If the weather outside is below thirty-two degrees Fahrenheit or zero degrees Celsius, be sure to limit your time outside to twenty minutes at a time.

Morkies love to play in the snow, but never let them play in the snow unsupervised.

In snowy areas, salt or other chemicals may be used on the sidewalks and roads to melt the ice and prevent us from falling or slipping. It can cause damage to your pup's paws.

For this reason, it is recommended during the snowy season to put waterproof booties on its paws. Or you can purchase a product called paw wax at your local pet supply store. This will protect your best friend's little paws.

Hot weather: Morkies have a hard time in extreme heat. For temperatures above eighty-five degrees Fahrenheit or thirty degrees Celsius, it would be wise to limit your dog's time outside to twenty minutes at a time. Try walking your dog earlier and later in the day, when the temperatures are more reasonable.

Morkies are prone to becoming overheated, which can lead to such serious complications as heat exhaustion or heat stroke.

When your Morkie is outside at the temperatures mentioned above, be sure to bring along some water for it to drink along the way. At your local pet supply store, you can buy a collapsible water bowl, which you can easily carry along.

Hot surfaces and pavement might not seem hot to you, but you are wearing shoes. For your Morkie, it is like walking on burning coals. Walking on hot surfaces can actually burn your puppy's paws. It is recommended to put little booties on your Morkie or purchase paw wax from your local pet supply store, to protect its little paws.

How much exercise does your Morkie need?

Just like humans, Morkies need to get about thirty minutes a day of exercise. It is highly recommended to give your Morkie two walks a day, each walk about twenty minutes long.

Exercise doesn't just mean walks. It can be playing fetch, hide and seek or any cardio activity. Keeping your Morkie active helps it release any extra energy that could cause bad behaviors such as barking or chewing on your furniture.

Can you over-exercise your Morkie?

Yes, you can over-exercise your Morkie. Normally a dog the size of a Morkie can walk at a normal pace, a few times a day for up to thirty minutes. But take into consideration that Morkie strides are very tiny when compared to yours. A thousand steps for you may be three thousand steps for your pet, so it can get tuckered out pretty fast.

Another factor to take into consideration is how vigorous the exercise is. Going for a ten-minute jog puts a lot of stress on its little tiny body and bones. Your Morkie will run with you as long as you do, but it will cause unnecessary stress on its body and cause future health concerns. Morkies are people pleasers so don't make it do more than it is able to do. Even though they are high-energy dogs, they don't have the same stamina as larger dogs to run long distances or climb mountains or stairs.

When is the best time to take your Morkie for a walk?

All dogs love to have a regular schedule, especially Morkies. They have a wonderful internal clock, which helps them remember precisely when it is time to eat, go to the bathroom, sleep or play. They get very disappointed when exercise or playtime is cancelled.

You can decide the schedule that works best for taking your little puppy outside for a stroll. Many pet owners find one walk in the morning and another after dinner works best for them. Try to avoid walking your dog too close to bedtime, as it will be very excited and have a difficult time going to bed.

Indoor games that your Morkie will love

There will be days that being outside longer than five minutes will be almost unbearable because of the freezing cold. But there is still a good way to burn off excess energy, by playing games inside your house. One game every Morkie just adores is Hide-and-Seek; they could play this game for hours.

How can you play Hide-and-Seek with your dog?

Many dogs will just play Hide-and-Seek with you, no toys needed. But other dogs need to see a toy to begin playing. When playing with a toy, make sure your puppy sees where you hid it, such as under the couch or a small pillow on the floor. Then act like you are looking for it too and your Morkie, being very intelligent, will find it for you. Then generously praise it. Once it has mastered this part of the game, you can make it more challenging by making your Morkie sit far away as you hide the toy, or show it the toy, then hide it in the other room, and ask your Morkie to find it.

Another game is to play with an ice cube on the kitchen floor. This will fascinate your puppy until it has totally melted. This is a great game during the hot summer months and for teething puppies.

Rule of thumb: Whatever games you decide to play with your puppy, inside or outside, make sure it doesn't have to jump up or down, as Morkies are prone to slipped kneecaps and hip joints.

CHAPTER SEVEN
Your Morkie's dietary needs

"Morkies, like most other toy dogs, have lots of teeth in small little mouths. It is important they get plenty of good crunchy food to help keep their teeth clean."

Pam Peterson
www.royalkennels.com

Your Morkie is a small dog that loves to eat, as do most dogs. Most of us have heard the following expression: "You are what you eat." The meaning of this expression is that if we eat healthy foods, we will be healthy but if we eat unhealthy foods, we will be unhealthy. This is a basic truth that cannot be denied.

Literally, all living creatures are made up of cells produced from what we eat. As humans, food can affect how we feel, our appearance, overall health, moods and weight. In the last few years, we have discovered the importance of eating whole foods and avoiding all types of processed foods.

Your Morkie will only be as healthy as the food you decide to feed it. Most people would just pick up a bag of dry dog food at the supermarket and not even give it a second thought. But is that really healthy? Do you know what you are feeding your dog?

In this chapter we will discuss how the food you feed your Morkie will have a direct effect on its future and its physical health. You want to give your Morkie the best life possible, so how can you take care of its nutritional needs correctly?

Daily nutritional needs

Both humans and dogs need certain basic nutrients in order to survive. Dogs need water, protein, carbohydrates, minerals and vitamins.

Morkie puppies have a faster metabolism than adult Morkies, so their nutritional needs differ slightly. Puppies will need to eat more often than adult dogs because they have a smaller tummy and can't hold much food.

During your Morkie's first two years, it needs to receive the proper nutrients to ensure proper bone growth. During the first two years of its life, your Morkie is growing extremely fast and will burn more calories than an older dog. This is why it is so important for it to receive the correct amount of nutrients, minerals and vitamins needed to grow in a healthy way.

Human dietary needs change during different stages of our lives, depending on our age, etc. Dog dietary needs also change according to the stage of their lives.

The food you feed your dog must include:
1. Energy that comes from carbohydrates
2. Protein
3. Fats, including fatty acids
4. Vitamins, minerals and micro-nutrients

How much and when

If dogs ruled the world, they would eat non-stop twenty-four hours a day. Have you ever noticed how your dog devours its meal in seconds, and then looks up to you begging for more food? All dogs love to eat and would probably eat themselves to death, if they could. They don't understand when to stop eating, and your little Morkie is no exception to that rule.

You might think you are doing your Morkie a favor by giving it tons of snacks and treats because it is so happy when it is eating. Overfeeding your Morkie can cause it to become overweight or even obese, and once that happens, health problems such as diabetes and heart disease begin.

How much your Morkie needs to eat each day will depend entirely on its size, age, build, metabolism and activity level. As every snowflake is unique, so is every dog; every Morkie is one of a kind, so they will not all require the same amount of food.

If your Morkie is extremely active it will need more calories than a Morkie that spends its time lying around all day on the couch. Another factor to be taken into consideration is the type of food you are feeding your dog; a general rule of thumb is the higher the quality of the food you feed your dog, the less it will need. But the cheaper and poorer quality food means more food because of all the fillers it contains, which mean unnecessary calories for your dog.

Rule of thumb: Dogs are not like cats; with some cats you can leave their dish full all day long and they will not overeat. But with dogs the temptation is just too great and they will devour it. Leaving your Morkie's food dish full guarantees that your dog will be obese.

<u>How can you tell if your Morkie is overweight?</u>

1. Look at your Morkie over and check out its waistline. Your dog shouldn't look like a long log or a sausage. Its shoulders should be wider and its back should begin to narrow towards the waist and hips.

2. Now place your hands on its back along the spine. Can you easily feel the ribcage? You should be able to feel it without pressing too hard. If you can't feel the ribcage, it is a warning sign that your Morkie is overweight and needs a diet with exercise.

Rule of thumb: Never get into the habit of feeding your Morkie from the table. This teaches bad behavior and encourages it to over-eat and beg for food. Make sure your whole household is on the same page with this rule.

How often should your Morkie be fed?

Adult dogs should be feed twice daily, once in the morning and once in the evening. Normally your Morkie should be fed around your break-fast and dinner times. This helps you to monitor its daily intake be-cause its routine is similar to yours. This also helps it to be regular in going to the bathroom.

Puppies should eat three to four times a day until they are nine to twelve months old. They have an extremely fast metabolism and they're burning calories at an incredible rate.

Rule of thumb: Make sure your dog has access to fresh water all day, every day.

How much is too much?

As mentioned above, it depends on your Morkie's age and how active it is the amount of food it should eat.

Most dog food bags or cans come with instructions as to the correct portion to feed your dog according to size, weight and activity level. Be sure to read the instructions on your selected dog food before feeding your dog.

Here is a basic chart to help understand how much food your Morkie should be eating daily. The amounts given are just a guideline and you will need to take into account your Morkie's age, metabolism and activity level.

DOGS WEIGHT	AMOUNT PER DAY
3 pounds	1/3 cup to 1/2 cup
5 pounds	1/2 cup to 2/3 cup
10 pounds	3/4 cup to 1 cup
20 pounds	1 1/4 cups to 1 3/4 cups

Please, remember this chart is a basic guideline to help give you a general idea of your Morkies food requirements.

Most adult dogs will eat only twice a day, so you will need to divide the above mentioned portions in half for their two meals a day.

Commercial dog food vs. homemade dog food

A couple of years ago, there was a major recall of dog food in the United Sates because it was laced with melamine. Melamine is a deadly industrial chemical that causes kidney stones, kidney failure and finally death in humans and animals. The FDA has not approved the use of melamine in any type of food products for animals or human consumption. This giant recall caused many pet owners to wake up and smell the coffee, to start paying more attention to what they are feeding their dogs. Many decided to start making homemade dog food.

Let's see how commercial dog food compares to homemade dog food.

The FDA Center for Veterinary Medicine requires that pet food be "pure and wholesome" and "safe to eat for animals" but the pet food does not need approval from the FDA before being placed on the shelves to purchase. This allows the commercial pet food companies a huge lee-way in what is put into their pet food.

Many pet food companies use the same expression on their ingredient list: by-products. What are by-products exactly? They can be ground up sick animals, blood, chicken beaks and feet. The ingredient list may state that it contains vegetables, but if not specified exactly what vegetables are used, it is most likely fillers such as corn or beet pulp that are unhealthy for dogs.

Plus the FDA allows certain additives and preservatives to be used in animal feed that are considered to be unsafe for human consumption. Many of these additives have been proven to cause very serious health problems such as cancer, kidney failure, liver failure and much more.

Homemade dog food is actually "wholesome and pure" and "safe to eat for animals" because you know what is in it. You aren't giving your pet ground up sick animals or fillers that are full of sugar. You are able to choose high quality ingredients that you would eat.

Home-cooked food doesn't have any unnecessary preservatives or additives, as it is made fresh then quickly frozen for your Morkie to enjoy in the next few days. It didn't come from a bag that has been sitting on your grocery store's shelf for the last two years.

Why do the commercial dog food manufacturers use fillers? They use them to bulk up the food, so it looks like you are getting more for your money. Also, it makes your dog full, but full of fake food that doesn't have any real nutrition.

Ask yourself the following questions: "Would I eat my dog's food? Would I serve it to my family?" Most of us would answer "No," as we reason that it isn't healthy. If we wouldn't eat it, why should we give it to our pets?

If you decide to purchase a commercial dog food, ask yourself while reading the ingredient list if you would eat that. If you would, then it is safe to feed your Morkie. You want to give it the best, and the best dog food probably isn't what's on sale at the supermarket. You will likely have to buy it at your local pet supply store or order it online

Photo Courtesy of
Michele Locricchio

Advantages to choosing a wholesome commercial brand dog food:

There are some amazing commercial dog food brands on the market today, but you will probably not find them at your supermarket; you'll have to go to your local pet supply store or you can order them online from a reputable retailer. When choosing a commercial brand dog food, look for brands that use whole foods and avoid using chemicals, preservatives and artificial flavors.

- **Convenience:** There is no preparation or cleanup needed. You just need to put it in your pup's dish and voila, dinner is served.

- **Training:** With obedience training, quite a bit of food is used and it is easier to use a pre-bought treat or dry kibble than to offer a handful of stew or mush. You can keep these treats out at room temperature and in your pocket, so you can easily reward your pup every time it responds correctly.

- **Peace of mind:** Home-cooked food can be an extra stress and anxiety as pet owners might wonder if their dog is receiving the correct balance of nutrients needed to grow and develop. Also, they may wonder if their dog is getting its basic daily requirements.

- **Cost-efficient:** Time is money. Not all of us have extra time to make our dog homemade dog food. Also, the homemade dog food will only be as healthy and wholesome as the ingredients we use and using high-quality meats and organic free-range chicken quickly adds up in price.

Disadvantages of choosing a commercial brand dog food:

This is mostly referring to generic brands that are commonly found at your supermarket, not the high-quality brands that you can find at pet supply stores. These are commercial brands that are jam-packed with ingredients that you can't even pronounce.

- **Bloat:** Many generic dog food brands contain fillers that can cause your Morkie to become bloated and gassy. If you find your dog suffers from bloat, it might do better with a wet food diet such as canned food.

- **Mundane:** Even though your dog only has around 1,700 taste buds and we humans have more than 9,000, it can be boring to eat the same thing every single day.

- **Health:** Many of the ingredients are fillers, sugar, and ground up animals that might have been sick with tumors and other diseases. Also, they use artificial flavors, chemicals and preservatives that can cause your pooch to have behavioral and physical issues.

- **Obesity:** Many dogs suffer from obesity, which leads to other health problems. It is hard to control your Morkie's weight with a generic commercial dog food, as many of the ingredients are jammed-packed with sugar and trans-fats.

Advantages to a homemade dog food:

- **Peace of mind:** You know exactly what you are feeding your dog, as you are the chef. It is made fresh, so the ingredients haven't lost their nutritional value. By controlling the ingredients, you control your Morkie's exposure to chemicals and other harmful additives.

- **Allergies:** If your puppy suffers from food allergies, you can control its exposure to these foods.

- **Cost-efficient:** Many pet owners who decide to make their own dog food use ingredients that they purchase for their family. Also, they make their dog's meals at the same time they make their family's meals, making it more cost-efficient and less time consuming.

Disadvantages of homemade food:

- **Daily nutrition concerns:** Many pet owners that make their own dog food often worry if their dog is receiving the correct amount of daily nutrients in its diet. Some studies have shown that dogs that are fed a homemade dog food diet suffer from nutritional deficiencies because of lacking nutrients.

- **Shelf life:** As all the ingredients are fresh, they tend to spoil fast and encourage bacterial growth and food-borne illness.

- **Costly:** Depending on the ingredients you use, it can become quite costly to make your Morkie's food.

Choosing whether to feed your Morkie a commercial brand dog food or a homemade dog food is your decision. Never let anyone pressure you into doing something that you are not 100 percent convinced about. Your Morkie is your pet and your responsibility. You need to decide what diet and food fits your schedule and allows you to give your Morkie the best life possible.

How to choose a wholesome commercial dog food

Have you ever stopped to look at the ingredient list on the common dog food brands we find at the supermarket? It's easy to choose a dog food brand because you trust the name--maybe you even saw your parents buy that brand of dog food for your childhood dog. But is really wholesome?

Many of the mainstream dog food companies have learned how to cut corners in producing pet food and are out to make money; they are not concerned about your Morkie's health.

Here is a list of ingredients that you need to avoid at all costs. If you see that a dog food contains one or more of these ingredients, return it to the shelf and look for a different brand.

1. **BHA or BHT:** BHA is short for butyrate hydroxyanisole and BHT is short for butyrate hydroxytoluene. Why should they be avoided? They are both harmful preservatives used to extend the shelf life of commercial dog food. These two ingredients are considered to be harmful because they have been directly linked to kidney and heart damage and cancer.

2. **Meat by-products:** What does "meat by-products" mean? The FDA only requires for animal feed that contains "meat by-products" that the by-products be from any animal source. What does this mean? It can be a mixture of anything from animal eyes, hooves, feet, beaks, feathers, blood, sick animals and any other kind of animal waste. Many times the sick animals that are ground up into the mixture have tumors or other illnesses. Also, other dead animals are thrown in there, such as dead dogs from local shelters.

   Exception: Only buy the commercial dog food if the packaging specifies that the by-products have been made from human-grade organ meats, such as livers and kidneys.

3. **Ethoxyquin:** Ethoxyquin is a pesticide and food preservative that has been banned for human consumption, as it has been directly linked to causing cancer. It is, though, commonly used as a preservative in commercial dog foods that contain fishmeal. A scary fact about ethoxyquin is that manufacturers are not required to include it on the ingredient list.

   Exception: When looking for a dog food that contains fish, look for a written guarantee that it doesn't contain ethoxyquin. It should be on the packaging or their website. If it doesn't have a written statement, it is likely that it contains ethoxyquin, so put it back on the shelf.

DAVID Anderson | Complete Guide to Morkies

4. **Corn:** Yes, corn! Corn is a cheap filler that has almost no nutritional value and can easily develop fungus or mold, causing your little Morkie to become very sick.

5. **Propyl Gallate:** It is also called Gallic Acid and Propyl Ester; this ingredient has been linked to liver disease and cancer.

6. **Corn syrup:** Corn syrup is harmful for your dogs as well as yourself. It is used to sweeten commercial dog food to mask the flavor of the chemicals and by-products. It is an unnecessary ingredient that has absolutely no nutritional value. It can also cause your dog to become addicted to sugar and sweets leading to unwanted weight gain, diabetes, tooth decay, behavioral problems and hyperactivity.

7. **Soy:** It is another cheap filler used to boost the protein content in low-quality dog food. Soy has been linked to harming the canine endocrine system.

8. **Artificial colors and flavors:** We all know that artificial colors and flavors are bad for us, and even more so for our dogs. Any ingredient list that has the word "artificial" in it should be avoided, as it is unnatural. Artificial colors and flavors have been linked to cancer and mental and behavior issues.

This is just the tip of the iceberg when it comes to harmful ingredients being used in commercial dog foods. It pays to invest in a higher-quality dog food as you will know exactly what you are feeding your dog. You will save money in the long run because it will not suffer from health-related ailments caused by its diet.

How to choose a high-quality commercial brand dog food:

It can be overwhelming choosing a dog food, but this list will help you look for a wholesome brand.

1. **Superior source of protein:** The main ingredient on the label should be a single source of protein, such as chicken meal or beef meal. Avoid poultry meal or meat meal, which are too vague and will be lower-quality protein.

2. **Whole-meat source as the first two or three ingredients:** Example: Chicken, chicken meal or Beef, beef meal. A good mix of meat proteins helps round out your Morkie's amino acids.

3. **Whole, unprocessed grains and vegetables:** The more processed the food, the less nutritional value it has.

4. **Expiration date:** Look at the date of production and the date of expiration. If it has a shelf life of two or more years, put it back on the shelf and move on to a different brand.

130

5. **Ingredient list:** The longer the list, the faster you need to get away from that brand of dog food.

6. **Canned dog food:** Canned dog food might be more expensive, but it is a great option. It has the highest nutritional value and contains high-quality cuts of meat. Often it contains hardly any preservatives or chemicals.

How to make a wholesome homemade dog food

Many pet owners opt to make homemade dog food but supplement by using a high-quality dog food to ensure that their dogs are receiving the correct nutrients. You will find some scrumptious recipes at the end of this chapter that your Morkie will love.

Photo Courtesy of Tami Mclaughlin

What are the correct proportions for a homemade dog food recipe?

- **40 - 50% protein:** Poultry, beef, lamb, fish or pork. Up to ten percent of this can be organ meats such as liver or hearts. Make sure the protein you use is high-quality and fresh.
- **25 - 30% vegetables:** Make sure they are well-cooked and finely chopped; dogs have a hard time digesting raw vegetables. You can use green beans, carrots, peas, broccoli, spinach and sweet potatoes.
- **25 -30% starch:** Brown or white rice, oats or pasta. If your Morkie is gluten intolerant, you can use gluten free pasta.

When choosing a recipe to for dog food make sure none of the ingredients are toxic for your Morkie. If you are unsure, just check the list of foods to avoid found in this chapter. Also make sure that the recipe follows the proportions mentioned above for proteins, vegetables and starches.

Tips for making homemade dog food

Here are some helpful tips for making homemade dog food:

1. After reading the information above about the threats found in commercial dog food, you may want to begin to feed your dog home-made meals immediately. Changing your dog's food too fast can cause it to have diarrhea or an upset tummy.

   Switch your Morkie's dog food slowly! Gradually switch the diet by mixing the new homemade food with the old commercial dog food. Slowly phase out the processed food.

2. Take time to prepare your dog food. Find a time to make the meals and give yourself time to put everything in freezer bags, measured in appropriate portions for your dog. Just as when cooking for your family, use safe food handling practices, especially if using raw meats.

3. Buy ingredients in bulk, as it will save you money, resulting in your homemade dog food not being more expensive than the commercial dog food.

4. Buy organic and high-quality ingredients. The meals will only be as wholesome as the ingredients you use. Choose good high-quality meats and organic chicken, whenever possible.

5. You can prepare the homemade dog food in larger batches and just freeze it in daily portion sizes, saving time and energy.

6. Many Morkie owners who have chosen to make home-cooked meals for their dogs also give them a multivitamin. Ask your veterinarian to recommend a multivitamin or supplement for your dog.

7. An important point to remember is portion control. Even though homemade food is wholesome and healthy, too much of a good thing can cause weight gain, which will lead to future diseases.

When choosing a home-cooked meal, observe whether your Morkie enjoys eating it. It doesn't matter how nutritious the meal is, if it goes un-eaten it serves no nutritional value for your Morkie. Make food that is healthy but delicious for your little bundle of fur.

Here is a list of foods commonly used in homemade dog food:

- Whole eggs
- Carrots, cooked until tender
- Chicken, turkey, beef and pork without the fat
- Oats
- Sweet potatoes
- Salmon
- Peanut butter
- Plain yogurt
- Cottage cheese
- Pumpkin
- Apples, without the seeds
- Green beans

Why should you consider making your Morkie's meals?

There are many reasons to begin making your Morkie's dog food. One reason is that it can be cheaper and healthier than commercial dog food. Plus in the last few years it has been brought to light how many dangerous additives and by-products are being added to dog food.

In recent years many veterinarians have noticed a spike in food in-tolerances in dogs that have been directly linked to commercial dog foods. Many veterinarians and pet owners have noticed an imme-diate improvement when switching from commercial dog food to a homemade dog food diet.

Feeding your dog is no more difficult than feeding your child. You just need to know some guidelines of how to feed them and what not to feed them.

One main reason many dog owners decide to make home-cooked meals is because they love their dogs. Just like family, they want them to have long, healthy lives.

Ask yourself:

- Would you consider serving your family, especially the little ones, only canned and processed foods?
- Would you feed them the same thing every day?

Most of us wouldn't even consider that, because we know it isn't healthy and will cause health problems in the future. So why would we only feed our dog canned and heavily processed dog food?

All living creatures need to eat fresh, wholesome foods that are appropriate for their species. Logically speaking, would dogs find dry dog food and canned food in their natural habitat?

Many of the commercial dog foods on the market have been created for convenience and are so popular because of mass advertising.

We could compare these processed dog food companies to the many fast-food establishments that surround us in our neighborhoods. Yes, they are convenient, but are they healthy? How would our health be if we ate there every single day?

The answer is simple; we would be in dire need of a doctor in no time.

Maybe your lifestyle doesn't allow making your Morkie homemade dog food, but do try some of the fantastic biscuit recipes in this chapter for your four-pawed best friend. They will be a big hit.

Photo Courtesy of Teresa Hutchens

Foods to avoid

What foods should my dog never eat?

There are certain foods babies and toddlers shouldn't eat because those foods can cause damage to their bodies. Their stomachs cannot properly digest them, causing pain and discomfort. The same is true for dogs. Just because we love a certain food doesn't mean they should eat it.

Some foods that we enjoy can actually act as poison for our dogs. Here is a list of foods that you should never feed your dog:

- **Chocolate**: a little bit of chocolate can cause havoc in your dog's metabolic system causing it to vomit and have diarrhea. A large amount can lead to heart failure and finally death.
- **Garlic, onions, leeks and chives** can be very toxic for dogs. They can cause dogs to have anemia, making them very weak which causes them to have an elevated heart rate and to collapse.
- **Cinnamon** can irritate the inside of your dog's mouth causing sores. Also, it can lower the blood sugar, and lead to diarrhea, vomiting and liver disease. If your dog inhales it in powder form it can cause respiratory distress.
- **Raisins and grapes** can lead to kidney failure as they contain a toxin that causes severe liver and kidney damage.
- **Almonds, pecans, macadamia nuts and walnuts** are toxic for dogs. Macadamia nuts are the most poisonous, affecting the nervous system. Almonds can tear the esophagus and windpipe.
- **Salt** increases water retention, which leads to heart disease and failure.
- **Alcohol** can cause intoxication, lack of coordination, poor breathing and can lead to a coma or death.
- **Cooked bones** of any kind can easily splinter when chewed by your dog causing damage to the esophagus and windpipe. Raw bones are good for your dog's health and teeth.
- **Coffee** has the same effect on your dog as chocolate does.
- **Corn on the cob** blocks your dog's intestines and will have to be removed surgically.
- **Yeast,** on its own or in dough, can cause flatulence and discomfort; too much will cause the stomach to rupture.
- **Xylitol** is a sugar substitute in many food items today. It has no effect on humans but it is a toxin for your dog. The smallest amount can cause seizures and death.

- **Sugar,** in small amounts, is tolerable but too much sugar can lead to obesity, dental problems and diabetes.
- **Plums, peaches, pears and persimmons** can be a choking hazard. Also, pear seeds contain arsenic and peach pits when metabolized turn into cyanide.
- **Liver** is fine in very small doses but in large quantities it can cause adverse effects on your dog's muscles and bones.
- **Avocados** contain a toxin that causes dogs to have diarrhea, vomiting and heart congestion.

An excellent suggestion would be to make sure the whole family understands what your dog cannot eat. This will prevent someone sneaking it a treat that could cause serious health damage or death.

Above is a partial list of foods that dogs cannot eat. If you are in doubt about a food item that is not on the list, please check with your veterinarian before giving it to your dog.

Simple recipes for your Morkie

Here is a small selection of wholesome dog food recipes that will have your Morkie licking its chops at the very thought of eating them.

SINFULLY DELICIOUS TURKEY OR CHICKEN DOG FOOD

Your Morkie won't know how to thank you for this delicious dog food. It will be devoured in seconds.

INGREDIENTS
- 1 1/2 cups of plain rice, uncooked
- 1 tablespoon olive oil
- 3 pounds of ground turkey or chicken
- 3 cups of spinach, rinsed and finely chopped
- 2 large carrots, shredded
- 1 medium sized zucchini, shredded; or 1 cup of shredded pumpkin
- 1/2 cup of peas, frozen
- 1/2 cup chicken or turkey broth, unsalted

INSTRUCTIONS
1. Cook the rice in a large pot according to the instructions on the packaging. Set aside.

2. In a pot, cook the ground turkey or chicken with the oil until fully cooked. While cooking, break up the ground meat to avoid large lumps.

3. Add the rest of the ingredients and cook together over low heat, until the broth has almost evaporated and the vegetables are fully cooked, about 10 minutes.

4. Add the rice and thoroughly mix together. Let cool completely.

DOGGY BEEF STEW

This will be one of your pup's favorite meals. It will have it licking its lips, even before it is served.

INGREDIENTS
- 1 pound of stewing beef, chopped to pea-size
- 1 small sweet potato, precooked and chopped
- 1/2 cup of carrots, diced small, precooked
- 1/2 cup of green beans, diced, precooked
- 1/2 cup of flour (or corn starch, if your dog is gluten intolerant)
- 1/2 cup olive oil

INSTRUCTIONS
1. In a large pot, cook the beef in one tablespoon olive oil until browned and dry. About 10 to 15 minutes.

2. Remove the cooked meat from the pot, reserving the drippings. Add the flour and the rest of the olive oil to the pot with the drippings. Whisk together over low heat until a thick gravy is formed.

3. Add the meat and the precooked vegetables. Stir until everything is evenly coated.

4. Serve cool.

RAW DOG FOOD RECIPE

Raw dog food can be easily digested by your dog and is very nutritious.

INGREDIENTS
- 2 1/2 pounds high quality sirloin steak, finely chopped
- 4 ounces of chicken livers
- 1 carrot, finely shredded
- 1 small apple, cored
- 1/2 cup of spinach, rinsed
- 2 whole eggs
- 1/2 cup plain yogurt or cottage cheese

- 1 tablespoon flax seed
- 1 tablespoon olive oil

INSTRUCTIONS
1. Place the carrot, apple and spinach into a food processor, and process until everything is finely chopped.
2. Add all of the remaining ingredients, except the chopped steak. Process again until everything is finely chopped and evenly combined.
3. Add all of the ingredients in a large bowl with the chopped steak. Mix everything together, using your hands.
4. Form into patties for your pup, taking into consideration its size, age and breed. Place on parchment paper and freeze until solid, then transfer to a sealable freezer bag.
5. The night before serving, take out a day's worth of patties and thaw in your fridge.

DOGGY CHILI

Your Morkie will love this protein packed meal that will keep it healthy and fit.

INGREDIENTS
- 4 organic chicken breasts
- 1 cup of kidney beans, rinsed and drained
- 1 cup of black beans, rinsed and drained
- 1 cup of carrots, finely diced or shredded
- 1/2 cup of tomato paste
- 4 cups of chicken broth, unsalted

INSTRUCTIONS
1. Cut the chicken into pea-sized pieces.
2. Place the chicken in a skillet and cook over medium heat with a small amount of olive oil.
3. Combine the cooked chicken with the other ingredients in a large pot. Bring to a boil and boil for 10 minutes or until the carrots are very tender.
4. Turn off the heat. Let cool, and freeze in daily portions for your puppy.

CROCK POT CHICKEN DOG FOOD

This will be one of your favorite recipes because it is so easy to make and will save you a load of cooking time, plus your pooch will love it.

INGREDIENTS

- 2 1/2 pounds of boneless, skinless chicken thighs and breasts
- 1 large sweet potato, diced in small pieces about the size of a pea
- 2 cups of frozen peas
- 2 cups of frozen green beans
- 1 large apple, cored and diced in small pieces about the size of a pea
- 1 can of kidney beans, rinsed and drained
- 2 tablespoons of olive oil

INSTRUCTIONS

1. Place the chicken in the slow cooker and cover with water just until it is covered. Then top with the sweet potato, carrots, kidney beans, green beans and apple.
2. Cook on low heat for 8-9 hours, when almost finished add the frozen peas. Cook for an additional 30 minutes.
3. Drain off the excess liquid; add the olive oil and mash together with a spoon, breaking up the chicken pieces.
4. Let cool. Scoop into daily serving portions and freeze in freezer bags. Thaw in the fridge overnight before serving.

SLOW COOKER PORK DOG FOOD

The minute you put this delicious meal in your puppy's dish, it will come running and devour it in seconds.

INGREDIENTS

- 3 pounds pork tenderloin
- 2 large yams, cut into large pieces
- 1 bag of peas, frozen
- 2 apples, peeled and cored
- 1 can of kidney beans, rinsed and drained
- 3 broccoli trees, broken into smaller pieces
- 2 cups of spinach, rinsed and finely chopped

INSTRUCTIONS

1. Place the meat in the slow cooker; add water until just covered.
2. Place on top the yams, apples, carrots, broccoli and beans. Cook on low heat for 7-8 hours or on high heat for 5-6 hours, add the frozen peas when almost done. Cook for 30 minutes more.

3. Add the finely chopped spinach right at the end and cook 10 more minutes or until the spinach is cooked. The pork should be able to shred apart easily. Mash the ingredients together.

4. Let cool. Scoop into portion-sized freezer bags and freeze. Thaw overnight in the fridge before serving.

DOGGY MEATLOAF

Everyone enjoys a good old-fashioned meatloaf and your pup is no exception. This meatloaf recipe will make your puppy smile all day long.

INGREDIENTS
- 1 pound of lean ground beef
- 2 eggs
- 1 1/2 cups of rolled oats
- 1/2 cups of cottage cheese
- 1 1/2 cups of mixed frozen vegetables

INSTRUCTIONS
1. Preheat oven to 350F.
2. Mix all the ingredients together until evenly combined; it is easiest to mix together by hand. Press into a greased loaf pan.
3. Bake for 40 minutes or until done.
4. Let cool. Cut into slices for easy serving. Freeze.

Biscuit recipes for your Morkie

We all love junk food and an occasional treat, but we realize the majority of the snacks on the market today are jammed-packed with chemicals, trans fats and extra calories. Most of us take the time to carefully read the ingredients before we choose a snack, avoiding ingredients that we are unable to pronounce.

Many parents have opted to just make homemade snacks for their children as a way to ensure that their children eat healthy. What about the commercial brand treats you buy for your Morkie? Should you be cautious?

As we have previously learned, many commercial brand dog foods use fillers, sugar and preservatives. Treats are no exception; actually, they cut even more corners with the treats, because there are no dietary requirements to take into consideration. Many brands use fructose, glucose and other sweeteners that your pup doesn't need.

There are some great doggy biscuits and treats on the market; you just need to do your research before you purchase a certain product.

But for those who have the time and desire to make doggy treats for your Morkie, here is a list of fast and easy recipes that your dog will love.

BACON PEANUT BUTTER TREATS

Bacon and peanut butter are every dog's favorite treat. You will have your pup begging for more of these delicious treats.

INGREDIENTS
- 1 cup of creamy peanut butter, unsalted and unsweetened
- 3/4 cup of milk
- 1 egg
- 2 cups whole wheat flour or a gluten free substitute
- 1 tablespoon baking powder
- 1/3 cup of whole oats
- 3 strips of bacon, cooked and chopped in small pieces

INSTRUCTIONS
1. Preheat the oven to 325F. Lightly grease your cookie sheets and set aside.
2. In a bowl, mix the peanut butter, milk, oats and eggs until thoroughly combined.
3. Add the flour, baking powder and bacon pieces. Mix until just combined. It will be a stiff dough and you might need to knead the dough to combine all the ingredients.
4. On a lightly floured countertop, roll out the dough about 1cm thick. Cut with a cookie cutter shaped like a bone (or any shape). Make sure the cookies are no bigger than 3cm. Arrange evenly on the cookie tray.
5. Bake for 18 to 20 minutes, then turn the cookies over and bake for 10 more minutes or until lightly browned. This will make a crunchy biscuit that will last a long time and be healthy for your Morkie's teeth.
6. Let cool before you give any to your pup. Store at room temperature for a week or freeze up to 3 months.

D.I.Y MORKIE ICECREAM

Ice cream, ice cream, we all scream for ice cream! Your Morkie pup will love these treats during the hot summer months.

INGREDIENTS
- 1 quart of plain yogurt
- 2 ripe bananas

- 1/2 cup of creamy peanut butter, unsweetened and unsalted

INSTRUCTIONS
1. Combine all the ingredients in a food processor. Pulse until smooth.
2. Place into small containers such as an ice cube tray and freeze.
3. Pop out of the containers and place in a freezer bag in the freezer.

JERKY CHICKEN OR BEEF CHEWS

This will be one of your pup's favorite snacks, especially when it is teething.

INGREDIENTS
- 2 pounds of chicken breasts or good-quality steak
- Oil, as needed

INSTRUCTIONS
1. Preheat oven to 200F.
2. Cut the chicken or steak into long thin strips, the thinner the better.
3. Lightly grease a rack with a cookie sheet underneath to catch the drippings. Evenly place the chicken or beef strips on the rack, allowing space around each one so they can dry our properly.
4. Cook in the oven for about 2 hours, then take then out and flip them over; cook for about 30 minutes to an hour more or until totally dried out. Some of the thicker pieces may take longer.
5. Store in the fridge or freeze.

NO BAKE PUPPY SNACKS

This is a perfect recipe for those hot summer days when you don't feel like turning on the oven.

INGREDIENTS
- 3/4 cup of creamy peanut butter, unsalted and unsweetened
- 2 ripe bananas, mashed
- 1 1/4 cup of rolled oats

INSTRUCTIONS
1. Cover a cookie sheet with plastic wrap and set aside.
2. In a bowl, mix all of the ingredients until thoroughly combined.
3. Form the mixture into balls, about 2cm in diameter. Place on the cookie sheet.
4. Chill the balls in the fridge for 1-3 hours or until firm. Store in a ziplock bag in the freezer.

BANANA CARROT TREATS

These biscuits are jam-packed with wholesome good-ness for your Morkie.

INGREDIENTS
- 1 cup whole wheat flour or a gluten-free substitute of your choice
- 1 cup oats
- 1 ripe banana, mashed
- 2 carrots, finely shredded
- 2 tablespoons olive oil
- 1 tablespoon brown sugar
- 1 tablespoon parsley, chopped
- 1 egg

INSTRUCTIONS
1. Preheat oven to 350F.
2. Place all of the ingredients in a bowl and mix until thoroughly combined.
3. On a lightly floured surface, place the dough and roll out till about 1/2 inch thick.
4. Cut into the desired shape using cookie cutters.
5. Place the cookies evenly on a lightly greased cookie sheet.
6. Bake for 30 minutes or less, depending on their size.
7. For a softer cookie, take out of the oven once baked. For a crunchy cookie, turn off the oven once baked and leave in the oven for 30 minutes more. This will dry out the cookie, making a crunchy snack for your puppy.
8. Let cool. Store at room temperature for one week or in the freezer for 3 months.

PEANUT BUTTER SANDWICH COOKIES

These snacks will get your puppy in the festive mood for the hol-idays. As they are more time-consuming to make, they can be for a special occasion.

INGREDIENTS
- 1 1/4 cup of flour, or a non-gluten substitute of your choice
- 1/2 teaspoon of baking powder
- 1/2 cup of creamy peanut butter, unsalted and unsweetened
- 1 egg

- 2 tablespoons of honey
- 1/2 cup of milk
- Additional creamy peanut butter, to sandwich the cookies together

INSTRUCTIONS

1. Preheat the oven to 350F.

2. In a bowl, place all of the ingredients together except the extra peanut butter for sandwiching the cookies together.

3. Mix everything together until thoroughly combined.

4. On a lightly floured surface, roll out the dough until about 1 inch thick. Cut into the desired shapes and sizes. Place on a lightly oiled cookie sheet.

5. Bake for about 10-12 minutes or until they have a uniform color. Cool.

6. Place in a freezer bag and freeze. Whenever you want to give your Morkie pup a festive treat, just smear some peanut butter on the bottom side of one of the cookies and sandwich together with another cookie.

7. It is recommended to sandwich the cookies together just before serving to prevent the cookies from getting soggy.

APPLE, CHEDDAR AND BACON BISCUITS

These scrumptious biscuits will be sure to get your Morkie to be the world's best-behaved dog. Its tail won't stop wagging while enjoying one of these treats.

INGREDIENTS

- 1 2/3 cups of flour
- 1 1/2 cups of whole wheat flour
- 1 egg
- 1/4 cup of softened butter or olive oil or a combination of both
- 1 large apple, cored and peeled, grated
- 2 tablespoons parsley, chopped
- 3 pieces of bacon, cooked and broken into small pieces
- 1 cup of cheddar cheese, grated
- 1 cup of milk

INSTRUCTIONS

1. Preheat oven to 350F.

2. In a bowl, place all of the ingredients and mix until thoroughly combined.

3. On a lightly floured surface, roll out the dough to about 1/4 inch thick.

4. If desired, as you roll out the dough, sprinkle extra cheese and bacon bits on top to make the treats look even more delicious.

5. Cut into the desired shapes for your Morkie's mouth. Place evenly on a lightly oiled cookie sheet.

6. Bake for 20 to 30 minutes, depending on the size.

7. Cool completely. Store at room temperature for one week or in the freezer for 3 months.

CHAPTER EIGHT
Morkies and their health

As Morkies are still considered to be a newer crossbreed there isn't a long list of aliments that have come to be associated with them. In this chapter we will discuss some common maladies that affect your Morkie's parents, the Maltese and Yorkshire terrier, and also some common health concerns that pop up occasionally with Morkies.

By understanding health issues that might come up in the future, you can take precautions to prevent them from developing. If they do occur, you can recognize the symptoms and take your Morkie to the veterinarian as soon as possible.

Vaccinations

The first order of business in preventive care is vaccinating your Morkie. Your veterinarian will explain the vaccination schedule. Normally, your veterinarian will give you a small handbook, which will have the age for first shots, future dates for booster shots and the length of immunity.

Below is a typical vaccine schedule for dogs; your veterinarian may use a slightly different one. Most veterinarians send out reminders to their clients before it time for vaccines.

Dog Vaccine Schedule	
Age	Vaccination
5 weeks	Parvovirus: Puppies are at high risk for this virus.
6 and 8 weeks	Combined vaccine: often called a 5-way vaccine for adenovirus cough, hepatitis, distemper, parainfluenza and parvovirus, it might contain leptospirosis and coronavirus.
12 weeks	Rabies: Might vary according to law in different states.
12 and 15 weeks	Combined vaccine: Containing leptospirosis, coronavirus and Lyme disease.
Adult (boosters)	Combined vaccine: Containing leptospirosis, coronavirus, Lyme disease and rabies

Vaccinations are divided into two different categories. The main ones are called "core vaccines." These are vaccines that every dog should receive. The second category is called "non-core vaccines." These are only recommended for certain dogs and certain parts of the United States.

If you plan on using a kennel or sending your Morkie to doggy day care, it might be wise to get the vaccine for kennel cough. Kennel cough is a horrible dry cough that is very contagious and is commonly spread in areas where there are lots of dogs, such as a kennel or doggy day care. Your dog can even catch it at the groomer.

For a more detailed explanation of the different vaccinations your Morkie will need, please talk to your veterinarian.

Neutering and spaying

Many Morkie owners decide to get their dogs neutered or spayed because Morkies are not a registered breed and aren't profitable for breeding. Also, second generation Morkies are not as attractive as first generation Morkies.

Spaying and neutering are simple procedures performed by your veterinarian, removing your dog's ability to reproduce. It is a very fast, simple and common operation for dogs.

Advantages to neutering your male Morkie:
- Less aggressive
- Less inclined to mark territory
- Less competitive
- More likely to form a tight bond with his human owner
- Less territorial

Advantages to spaying your female Morkie:
- They do not go into heat
- Less nervous
- Less barking and crying
- No unwanted pregnancies

Advantages for neutering or spaying your male or female Morkie:
- Less inclined to roam
- Less aggressive
- More calm and sedentary
- Less likely to escape

- More obedient

Medical studies have proven that dogs that have been neutered or spayed will have a lower risk of cancer, compared with dogs that haven't had these procedures.

Both spaying and neutering require general anesthesia.

Spaying and neutering will not affect your dog's personality. It will not resent you because of this operation; he or she will just carry on with life as before the operation. These procedures mellow out the unfavorable parts of their personalities, such as being aggressive.

What is neutering?

Neutering is a quick procedure that is performed by a licensed veterinarian surgeon. Once the operation is performed it will render your male dog unable to reproduce.

It is often referred to as castration because it removes your dog's testicles. It will leave an empty scrotal sac that previously contained your dog's testicles. Over time, this sac will shrink in size until no longer noticeable.

*Photo Courtesy of
Ivana Cox*

When should your Morkie be neutered?

It is recommended to neuter dogs before they are six months of age to avoid unwanted weight gain when they are older. Morkies that have been neutered after six months have the tendency to become quite obese.

Also, they will be less likely to wander if the operation is before they are six months old. Waiting until the Morkie is older than six months means your Morkie might have testosterone already built up inside of him. This testosterone will drive him to escape in search of a female to mate with.

Non-neutered males have the tendency to spray their pee around their living quarters, which includes your house. They do this to mark their territory; a neutered dog will not do this.

What is spaying?

Spaying is often referred to as sterilization for female puppies. It involves a very simple procedure performed by a licensed veterinarian surgeon. This operation will prevent your Morkie from becoming pregnant and stop her regular heat cycles.

Spaying is more complicated than neutering male dogs. It involves removing both ovaries and the uterus by making a small incision into your puppy's abdomen. The uterus is normally removed because it may be prone to infections in the future.

When should your Morkie be spayed?

Veterinarians suggest the best time is between four and six months of age. But it can be done later on with no side effects.

Health Concerns

Hopefully the only time you will need to see the vet is for your Morkie's yearly checkups, but in case your pet gets sick, it's helpful to know the warning signs of a serious condition. Following is a list of symptoms that warrant a call to the veterinarian.

When should you call your veterinarian?

- **Change in temperament:** Your pet shows unexplained changes in appetite or behavior, or is very lethargic.
- **Limping:** It might favor one paw over another, having a limp or swagger when it walks; refuse to stand up (even when bribed with a treat), or have difficulty walking.
- **Difficulty breathing**: If your Morkie looks like it is gagging or cannot breathe, check its airways and call your veterinarian.

Photo Courtesy of
Amy Cantley

- **Excessive drooling:** It is typical for some dogs to drool while watching you eat, but excessive drooling is when your dog drools for no apparent reason and doesn't stop.

- **Neurological conditions:** Your Morkie is normally alert and responsive. Suspect neurological problems if your dog becomes disoriented, unresponsive, uncoordinated or severely lethargic.

- **Seizures:** If your dog has never experienced a seizure before, it needs to see a veterinarian as soon as possible. Seizures could manifest as incontrollable shaking, tremors, loss of consciousness, or possibly loss of bowel control.

- **Toxic exposure:** If you know your dog was exposed to something toxic or a food item that is toxic for dogs, immediately take your dog to the veterinarian.

- **Vomiting and diarrhea:** If vomiting and diarrhea last longer than twenty-four hours, call your veterinarian.

- **Distended abdomen or abdominal pain:** If you notice your dog having dry heaves or retching, or it is weak, collapsing and having trouble breathing, it is likely your dog is suffering from bloat. It is more common in large dogs, but does occur occasionally with smaller dogs. This is a life-threatening problem if not quickly treated by your veterinarian.

Photo Courtesy of
Diana Minor

- **Urinary problems:** If you notice that your dog tries to go pee but is unable to, it might have a urinary blockage.

This is a partial list of some basic health issues that might require an emergency visit to the veterinarian's office. Your veterinarian has an emergency number for a reason, so don't be afraid to use it.

Future health concerns and how to prevent them

Below you will find some common illnesses that affect both the Yorkshire terrier and Maltese breeds; hence your Morkie may be prone to them. This list isn't meant to frighten you, but to prepare you and make you aware of them, and also teach you how to help prevent your Morkie from suffering from these ailments.

White Shaker Syndrome: This syndrome affects Maltese dogs and could be an issue for your Morkie. It normally manifests itself when your puppy is about six months old.

Symptoms: Your dog will have tremors all over its body, lack of coordination and rapid eye movement.

It doesn't cause your dog any pain and will not change your dog's personality. It will, however, give you a panic attack the first time it happens. It normally happens when the dog gets overly excited or stressed. Talk to your veterinarian about how to treat it. If you are unsure whether it has White Shaker Syndrome, film it on your camera and show it to your veterinarian.

Epilepsy: This is when your Morkie has seizures.

Symptoms: Your dog will begin to shake uncontrollably for a few seconds or longer. It is suspected to be hereditary, but this hasn't been scientifically proven yet.

Epilepsy cannot be cured but it can be treated effectively with medicine. If your Morkie has epilepsy, with good management, it can live a long and happy life with no complications.

Patellar Luxation: Also called "slipped stifles," this is a common problem for all small dogs. It is caused when the three parts of the patella, the thighbone, kneecap and the calf, are not properly lined up. This makes the leg become limp. It is considered to be a birth defect but doesn't present itself until later on in life. The rubbing of the unaligned bones can lead to arthritis or degenerative joint disease.

Symptoms: Walking with a limp, skip or hop. In severe cases, surgical repair might be required.

It is more common when good breeding practices aren't observed.

Porto-systemic shunt: Occurs when there is an abnormal flow of blood between liver and body. This becomes a problem because the liver is responsible for detoxifying the body, metabolizing the nutrients found in the food, and other things. Signs of this disease appear when your Morkie is around two years old.

Symptoms: Symptoms could be neurobehavioral abnormalities, such as lack of balance, lack of appetite, hypoglycemia, stomach issues and stunted growth.

Your veterinarian might recommend corrective surgery or a special diet.

Progressive Retinal Atrophy: This is a degenerative eye disorder that will eventually cause blindness. It takes years before your dog begins to go blind. It is inherited from the parents.

Symptoms: Your veterinarian can do a simple test to tell if your dog has this disease.

The good news is that dogs can use their other senses when they go blind and can live a happy and full life. This can be avoided of you do a physical background check on your Morkie's parents, since it is inherited. The breeder should have the paperwork proving that in the last five generations of your Morkie's family, there are no descendants that had Progressive Retinal Atrophy.

Good breeders will have their breeding dogs certified yearly and do not breed their dogs with dogs that carry this disease.

Legg-Calve-Perthes Disease: This is a common problem for toy dogs. The blood supply to your dog's hipbone is decreased and the head of the hipbone that connects to the pelvis begins to disintegrate.

Photo Courtesy of
Kim Moore

Symptoms: Normally manifests itself when your puppy is around four to six months old; it begins to limp and its leg muscles become stiff.

This condition can be corrected by surgery and the prognosis is very positive, as most dogs have almost no lameness, and if so, only when the weather changes.

Most of these health issues are hereditary, so before purchasing your Morkie, investigate whether its parents suffer from any of these issues. Both parents should have a clean bill of health from the Orthopedic Foundation for Animals for patella (knees) and a certificate from the Canine Eye Registry Foundation certifying that their eyes are healthy.

Also, look for breeders that don't begin to breed their dogs until they are two or three years old, as many of these diseases don't manifest until after two years of age.

How to choose a good veterinarian

The day you pick up your Morkie and bring it home, you make a promise to this adorable little puppy that you will give it the best life possible and care for its every need.

It will depend on you for all of its basic needs including its medical care. How can you choose a respectable veterinarian?

Before you choose a veterinarian, sit down and ask yourself what are some qualities you want in your Morkie's future medical doctor. Also, make a list of questions that you would like to ask regarding your puppy. You can ask the local shelter, breeder and other dog owners for references on any veterinarian you are considering.

Make sure the veterinarian you are considering is approved by the American Animal Hospital Association. Sadly, many animal clinics are not approved by A.A.H.A. This membership ensures a certain level of medical care for your Morkie.

When you meet the veterinarian, do you pick up a positive vibe? Does he or she seem to love animals or just tolerate them?

A good veterinarian should have some basic equipment, such as an x-ray, ultrasound, IV pumps, blood and eye pressure measuring tools, and be able to do basic lab tests. Also find out if any specialists work in the clinic.

Does the clinic staff seem knowledgeable and friendly? Do they like animals or just tolerate them? You will bring your pet here and you will be paying for a service; you should get what you pay for.

Make sure the veterinarian is available at all hours, in case of an emergency.

CHAPTER NINE
Common behavior issues

"A common mistake in bringing your new puppy home is giving the pup the run of the house. You will never get the pup potty trained that way"

Karen Dawn Thomas
www.angellinekennels.com

A puppy is not born to be evil or wicked. There is no such thing as a puppy born with the "X" gene that will turn it into a psychopath. But all puppies are influenced by their surroundings and their interactions with others. These surroundings and interactions can mold your Morkie in a positive or negative way.

Bad upbringing and bad training produce badly-behaved dogs and are the reason dogs have behavioral problems. There is no such thing as a defective dog.

Photo Courtesy of
Madia Sargent

154

How to stop your Morkie from having bad habits

For your Morkie to understand what is expected of it, you need to learn to communicate in a way that it is capable of understanding. The communication also needs to be consistent, not one day "yes," next day "no."

Your Morkie is very intelligent but it is unable to read between the lines. If you are not consistent with training your dog, you will be only confusing it, and it will not be able to know its limits or boundaries.

You might be reinforcing bad behaviors without realizing it. You need to learn to reward your dog for positive behavior and not bad behavior. Behavior that is not rewarded will slowly decrease and behavior that is rewarded will increase, so make sure you are rewarding the correct behavior.

Remember, a large number of dogs end up in shelters and are abandoned between one and two years of age because of these bad habits. This is when the cute puppy behavior becomes not-so-cute and can be very frustrating to the owner.

By applying these simple steps now, you will prevent bad behavior and heartache later on. It will lead to a long and happy life with your new-found best friend, your adorable little Morkie.

Jumping

Have you ever walked into a house and been greeted by an overly friendly dog that won't stop jumping on you? It is quite annoying, especially if you are wearing nylons or dress pants.

You really don't want your Morkie to jump on everyone that comes through the front door. The key is to stop your dog from jumping in the first place. If it already jumps, you will need to stop it from forming a bad habit. The good news is that this bad habit is a very easy one to correct.

How to stop your Morkie from jumping:

1. Ignore your dog while it is jumping. This might be hard to do when it is still a puppy because it looks so cute. Only praise and reward your puppy when it is not jumping.
2. Never, ever pet your Morkie when it is jumping. Petting is a type of praise and affection, which sends a message to its brain telling it that jumping is good behavior. This will reinforce the jumping.
3. Once you see that your puppy has all four paws on the floor, reward it and give it a treat for not jumping.

155

4. If you have taught your puppy the command to lie down, give the command and then give it a treat and lots of praise when it does.

5. Repeat the first three steps until you can walk into a room or the house without your puppy jumping on you or other people.

Some pet owners have taught their dogs to dance and when they begin to jump: they say the command "dance," and their Morkie does a little dance around the room. But that can be taught only once all the other basic commands have been taught.

Biting

Each year more than 4.5 million people in United States alone are bitten by a dog. Children are the number one victim of dog bites, followed by the elderly, and third, postal workers.

Approximately twenty people die each year from complications due to dog bites. Many of the dogs that bite someone (whether the bite was fatal or not) are euthanized.

Biting should be discouraged from the very first day you bring your Morkie home. Puppies begin biting to relieve their teething discomfort and their sore gums. Avoid playing aggressive games such as tug-o-war; instead play positive games such as fetch and train your dog to drop the ball in front of you.

Before learning how to teach your Morkie not to bite, we need to understand how they interact with each other. As puppies are just beginning to control their bodily movements, they are very awkward and don't quite understand their own strength.

Many times, while playing with fellow puppies, they might bite too hard. What does the other puppy do? It yelps out in pain and the fun time comes to a halt. If the puppy bites its mom too hard, it might learn a harsher lesson. That puppy will never, ever bite its Mom again!

Just as it learns that biting its mom, brothers and sisters is not a good idea, it needs to learn that it can't bite humans. Whenever it tries to bite you, say a firm "no," stop playing, and do not engage it until it calms down.

How can you discourage your Morkie from biting?
- When your puppy begins to bite you or something that you don't want it to bite, firmly say "No" and remove the item it was biting (or your hand). Replace it with an acceptable chew toy.
- If your puppy is overly persistent with biting and chewing, many trainers suggest the following technique to get it to stop biting. Put your thumb over your dog's tongue and gently hold the bottom part of its mouth with your four fingers. As you do this say "No" firmly,

and then release its mouth. Do not give it another chewing toy at this moment. Repeat this process as necessary.

- If your puppy is determined to bite at all costs, begin hand feeding it. This will get it used to your hands being near its mouth and it will associate human skin with mealtime and not biting. If it bites you, say "No" and close up your hand, then resume feeding once it has calmed down.

- Some dogs are so hyperactive they don't even realize they are biting. If this is the case, put Cheese Whiz or peanut butter on your hands and your puppy will want to lick it off. As it approaches to lick it off, tell it "Kisses," and it will begin associate the word kisses with licking your hands instead of biting.

- If it bites particularly hard, yelp sharply as a puppy would, let your hand go limp and stop playing. This will startle your puppy and it will stop biting you. If it continues biting you after two or three yelps, it is time to give your puppy a time out.

Chewing

Chewing is one of the most common bad habits for most puppies. No matter how cute your Morkie looks chewing on your shoes, you have to stop it. If you don't, you are reinforcing bad behavior. Right from day one, you need to teach your Morkie that it is only allowed to chew on certain items.

Puppies use their teeth to explore their surroundings. This is considered to be normal behavior but it quickly becomes unwanted behavior when it chews on your shoes or furniture. If unwanted chewing isn't corrected when your Morkie is still a puppy, it can lead to costly destruction of your personal property, medical problems and trust issues between you and your dog.

Something nobody likes to mention is the terrible teething period that your Morkie is going to go through. From your Morkie's four-month birthday till it is about six months of age, it will go through a painful teething period. Its gums and teeth are sore and irritated and chewing helps to relieve the discomfort. Here are some tips to get you both through this phase:

- Puppy-proof your home. Remove objects that your puppy might want to chew on, such as shoes, socks or anything that seems chewable.

- Encourage chewing on appropriate items. Each dog will have its own preference as to the type of chew toys. You will need to experiment until you find your puppy's favorite type of chew toys.

- Don't give your Morkie an old shoe to chew on; it will not be able to tell the difference between a new and an old shoe. It will think all shoes are fair game for chewing because you already gave it a shoe.

- If you find your puppy chewing on an inappropriate object, correct it by taking the object away and saying a firm "No" as you remove it. Then give it a chew toy. Praise it when it begins to chew on the toy. Over time, your Morkie will learn what objects it can chew on and what objects it is not allowed to chew on.

- You can also apply deterrent sprays to objects that you don't want your puppy chewing on, such as the furniture or kitchen table legs. This spray is non-toxic and leaves a disgusting taste in your dog's mouth, which will deter it from returning to that object to chew. It will learn to stay away from it. You can find a deterrent spray for chewing at your local pet supply store.

- A tired dog is less likely to chew. Engage your dog in lots of play; many times dogs begin to chew out of boredom.

Separation anxiety

Morkies thrive on human companionship. They quickly bond with their owners and depend on them for their every single need. That is what makes Morkies the world's best companion dog, but this quality can sometimes turn against you.

What is separation anxiety?

Separation anxiety is caused when a dog feels stressed from being separated from its owner. It feels anxiety that it may express in a number of vocal or destructive ways. No matter how your dog manifests its feelings, this is a serious condition that needs to be dealt with.

Here are some of the ways that your Morkie might release stress and anxiety:

1. **Destruction of your personal belongings:** It might go on a chewing frenzy, chewing on your couch pillows, the coffee table, or anything else it might find. Basically anything that is in its path will be chewed on, and if possible, devoured.

2. **Defecating and urinating inside your house:** This is one of the most unpleasant side effects of separation anxiety. It might go to the bathroom throughout your house because it is so upset and afraid of being abandoned by you.

3. **Barking and whining uncontrollably:** Your neighbors will hate you when this happens and secretly begin to look for a way to evict you

Photo Courtesy of
Laura Dvorak

and your dog from the building. No matter how exhausted your dog is, it will continue barking until someone comes to its rescue.

4. **Relentless scratching:** It might scratch at the doors, as that is where you're left and it reasons that if it can just get outside it can find you.

5. **Pacing:** Some Morkies become so worked up that they begin intense, persistent pacing, becoming even more worked up.

6. **Physical issues:** In severe cases, it might begin to pant excessively, which could lead to heart failure in extreme cases.

Allowing your dog to experience separation anxiety can damage your Morkie's physical, mental and emotional health. The only reason your dog is experiencing separation anxiety is because it misses you and that makes it become anxious and stressed out every time you leave your Morkie home alone.

Sadly, you might be the reason your dog suffers from separation anxiety. You encouraged it to notice you were leaving and made it miss you. In what ways might you have done this?

You might be making a big fuss every time you are about to leave. Then when you come home, you make a big fuss again, by ooh-ing and ah-ing and giving your Morkie treats. This actually is counter-productive. It stresses your Morkie out because you got it all excited before leaving and then left it hanging. When you came home and made a big deal, you highlighted the fact that you were gone.

When Morkies are still little puppies, owners have the tendency to smother them with attention and take them everywhere because their puppies are so cute and irresistible. They are almost never left alone and get used to being together. Then as they get older and a little bit bigger the adorable puppy charm begins to wear off and suddenly the owners stop spending so much time with them. They feel like they need to be with their owners at all times and don't understand why they are being left home alone. The owners have become their security blanket and they can't cope when left alone.

From the very first day you bring your puppy home, it begins to experience separation anxiety because of being separated from its litter or pack. You bring it home into strange new surroundings and you become the pack leader.

You put your new puppy in the den or crate and walk away, and it begins to cry. What do you do?

You go running and pick it up and tell it everything is okay. By doing that, you are rewarding it for an undesired behavior; you are teaching your puppy that crying works.

From day one, you need to begin to teach your Morkie that it's fine to be alone for short periods of time. Leave it alone for thirty seconds and only return when it stops barking or whining. You can only reward good behavior such as being quiet and settled.

When your puppy is outside of its den, it isn't necessary to entertain it non-stop; encourage it to play by itself. This will prepare it for when you leave it alone in the future.

Morkies dislike changes to their routines and that can cause them to have separation anxiety. That is when they become stressed and destructive.

The minute you bring your Morkie home, it begins to look to you as its pack leader, since its mother has disappeared and is no longer in the picture. How can you help it learn that you are the new pack leader?

Trust. Your Morkie needs to learn to trust you 100 percent and you need to show it that you trust it, too. Your trust allows it to have confidence in itself that you know it will behave when left alone. This trust will be reflected when you leave it alone; it will know that you will be coming back. Your puppy will realize that you haven't abandoned it and you will return.

Separation anxiety is an indicator of how well you have trained your dog in all other aspects of obedience training. If you have trained your dog well and it is well-behaved, the chances of it suffering from separation anxiety are greatly reduced.

How can you teach your Morkie to be left alone in the house, without having a breakdown?

- Training takes time. Take time daily to show your puppy what you expect and help it understand how it fits into your daily routine. Take every opportunity for training; two minutes here and there adds up to some high-quality training time.

- Teach your dog to lie on the floor. Slip out of sight and then come back. Each time you do this, increase the time you slip away and come back. Don't make a big deal each time. Just act normal, and your dog will begin realize that you haven't abandoned it and you always come back. This is a trust and confidence exercise.

- Your family and yourself need to establish that you are the pack leaders and your Morkie isn't in control. It will try to be in control by getting you to do things such as pet it.

  It might come up to you and nudge your hand to be petted. This may seem so cute that you can't resist petting it. But in dog terms, your Morkie was in control of the situation. Then when it faces a situation such as being left at home alone, it realizes it isn't really in control and stresses and begins to act out.

- Change can sometimes cause Morkies to experience separation anxiety. You can help your dog deal with change by shaking up your routine each day. We are all creatures of habit.

If your dog tends to follow you around the house, when you get up to go to another room and notice your pup stands up to follow you, just sit back down and it will too. Wait a bit and then go. Come in or out of the house through a different door. Put your shoes and bag in a different area. Your pup will notice these small changes, but they will be small enough to deal with. This will help its confidence in itself grow, as well as its confidence in you as the pack leader.

If you are crate training your Morkie, place the crate in the busiest part of the house and go about your activities. This will get it used to hearing the everyday noises and movements without the need to be in the center of it. It knows you are in charge as the pack leader and you will protect it.

- Get your pooch used to being left alone by lots of rehearsals. Walk out and return before it begins to cry or bark. Allow your dog to see you go through all of the movements of leaving, such as putting on your shoes and your jacket, and leave briefly. When you come back in, calmly and indifferently greet your dog and ask your pup to do a command for you such as shake a paw, and then give it a reward.

Suggestions to help your Morkie relax when you leave it alone:
- Leave on the TV or music in the background for your Morkie while you are out. Most dogs like background noise and it can help them to feel more secure.
- If you leave your puppy in a crate when you go out, try covering part of it with a blanket. This will feel more like a den and will make it feel secure and safe.
- Leave toys that are safe to use without supervision and will keep your puppy distracted for some time. Toys that have treats that are occasionally released are great because it keeps your pet mentally engaged and soon it will get tired and fall asleep.
- Before leaving your house, avoid giving your Morkie too much attention; all it is going to understand is that all that love and attention was abruptly cut off, causing it to go into panic mode.
- Hide treats around the house; this will keep it occupied and prevent it from becoming bored while you are gone.

Separation anxiety is a sign that your dog loves you and misses you, but it is also a red alert that you haven't correctly trained your dog. But if you put the above suggestions into practice, it will not become stressed out or frightened when you leave it alone. It will have learned that you are its trusted pack leader and that you would never, ever abandon it.

True love is based on trust and respect. May your relationship with your Morkie be one based on true love.

Socializing with other dogs

The world is made up of all kinds of different and quirky personalities; dogs often resemble their owners' personalities or sometimes your dog's personality is as unique as your own.

Some dogs, for one reason or another, become very antisocial or shy. Just like people that are antisocial or shy, it can be awkward meeting and talking to them. They mean to say or do the right thing, but somehow it comes across as strange and they might even say something accidently that offends us.

Some dogs seem to get in fights with bigger dogs no matter how tiny they are because they have never properly learned how to socialize with other dogs. Dogs that haven't learned to socialize with other dogs will most likely grow up to be shy and skittish around anything that moves.

You want a dog that is able to act like a gentleman or a little lady when exposed to other dogs. There is nothing more embarrassing than a dog that tries to attack other dogs or anything else that moves.

When is the best time to socialize your Morkie?

The best time to begin socializing your Morkie is while it is still a puppy. Puppies haven't developed any pre-established opinions or misconceptions about other dogs; they just see other dogs as fun playmates.

You will need to choose your Morkie's new acquaintances carefully, as you'll have to check beforehand if they have their vaccinations up to date. Make sure the dog you are going to introduce your puppy to will be a friendly dog, so the experience will be positive and it will want to meet more dogs.

How to socialize your dog with other dogs:

Walking your dog is one of the best opportunities to introduce your Morkie to other dogs, as the meet and greet is short and sweet. Another reason why it is a great moment to introduce your dog to other dogs is because they have both already released some of their built-up energy from sitting around the house, so they are more likely to be calm and submissive. Plus the meeting is on neutral ground, so neither dog will be on the defensive side.

Tips for when your Morkie meets a new dog:
1. If your Morkie begins to bark at the other dog, don't pull back on the leash. That will get it even more excited and make it think it needs to protect you, turning this casual meeting into a negative, aggressive experience that your puppy will not forget.
2. If your dog begins to bark, do show a calm and assertive attitude and distract it to look somewhere else. If it doesn't stop barking just pick it up and walk away. There will be another chance to meet other dogs.

The dog park is one of the best places to introduce your Morkie to other dogs, but it can be extremely intimidating for your Morkie. Expose it slowly to the dog park. The first week, you might walk around the park but not go in. All the dogs are having fun inside the park and your Morkie will want to play with them. Each time you go back, go a little further inside, until you know your dog will not act antisocial, barking and trying to start a fight with the other dogs.

*Photo Courtesy of
Nicole Duckworth*

Socializing with all types of people

Have you ever walked into someone's house and were suddenly bombarded with a hyperactive dog jumping and barking at you? You probably didn't think too highly of the owner's dog-training skills. Other people's dogs are lurking around in the background as if they can't be trusted and are looking for the perfect opportunity to bite your ankles. Some dogs just run and hide under the couch or bed until the guests have left.

Nobody wants a pet that acts like the dogs mentioned above. So how can you teach your puppy to behave around strangers?

You need to teach your Morkie not to be prejudiced against anyone. Some dogs are wary of certain physical features, such as a beard, a cane, a hat or sunglasses. Others dislike anyone wearing a uniform, such as the postman.

Some Morkies even notice skin color and react suspiciously. The only way to prevent your puppy from acting with prejudice toward anyone is to introduce it to all kinds of people, men and women, of different races and appearances, when it is still a puppy.

Many dogs and puppies are wary around children. Instead of seeing them as cute mini-humans that giggle, they see them as strange creatures with loud voices, jerky movements and melodramatic emotions. Children frighten some dogs.

One of the saddest realities about dogs and children is that 60 percent of dog bite victims are children. Seventy-five percent of these bites are to the face. The only way to keep your dog from becoming part of those statistics is to socialize your dog with children from an early age.

Plan to begin socializing your Morkie from a very early age, just make sure that you supervise any interactions your dog has with children or other people. Even as your Morkie turns into an adult, it is important to continue socializing with children, as dogs can quickly forget how to act around children.

How to do a meet and greet with someone new:
1. Carry some treats in your pocket to reward your puppy after it meets someone new and acts properly. You can also give the new person some treats to share with your dog.
2. Ask the person to sit down and place your Morkie nearby. Tell the person to just ignore your puppy.
3. Let your Morkie make the first move. If it is interested and begins to smell the new person, the person can give your pup a biscuit and try to pet it.

4. Avoid sudden movements that might frighten your puppy.

5. Praise your puppy after it has made friends with the new person.

6. If your puppy seems skittish and uneasy, repeat the introduction another day until it is relaxed with the new person.

Let your Morkie be multicultural by letting it meet as many different types of people as possible. The more people it has interactions with, the better-behaved it will be in all types of social conditions.

Encourage polite children to pet your Morkie and maybe even give it a treat. Let it meet and greet people in wheelchairs, delivery people, people with deep voices, nuns, even homeless people that you encounter on walks.

The key is teaching your Morkie that there is nothing to be fearful of; everyone is a friend and they don't want to hurt either of you.

Learning to accept the postman

Dogs hate mail carriers. That remark might seem a bit cliché but it's true. Dogs dislike postal workers, FedEx delivery people and even the pizza delivery person. Why do they dislike these people so much?

Dogs, especially small dogs, dislike anybody walking up to the front door. They feel it is a threat and that it is their duty to protect their owners from this dangerous person knocking on the front door. Their defense mechanism kicks in and they begin to bark incessantly.

Here are some reasons why your Morkie dislikes your friendly neighborhood letter carrier:

1. **Territorial instinct:** Morkies can become quite territorial and from your dog's point of view, these people are invaders trespassing on its private property.

2. **Repeat offense:** Your dog is pleased, because the mail carrier appears to have listened to its warning barks and growls--after all, he or she left! But try to imagine how your dog feels when the same person comes back the very next day and the day after, etc. Your dog takes the daily visit from the postal worker as a recurring personal insult.

3. **Chemical release:** Whenever your dog is provoked and angry, its brain releases several hormones or chemicals which are addictive. This chemical release rewards your dog for the repeated bad behavior towards to mail carrier.

4. **Habit formation:** If your dog's aggressive behavior towards the mail carrier isn't corrected, it becomes generalized to anyone approaching the front door, and any noises that your dog doesn't like such as a honking vehicle. Allowing your dog to bark at the letter carrier can lead to behavior issues later on in life that will be very difficult to correct.

How can you teach your Morkie to like the mail carrier?

As with all behavioral training, it is best to start early in your puppy's life. If possible, introduce your Morkie to your mail carrier from day one. Put a treat in the mailbox and ask the mail carrier to knock on the door to meet your new puppy. Postal workers are generally eager to avoid getting bitten in the future, so they will happily meet your dog. This will teach your puppy that the mailman is a friend and it will be eager to welcome them to the house.

Another practical suggestion to introduce your Morkie to the mail carrier is to organize the meet and greet on neutral ground. Before the mail arrives at your house, put your dog on a leash and meet the letter carrier a few houses down from yours. Slip them a treat to give your Morkie and then walk to your door together. Your Morkie won't even realize that it is becoming friends with the mail carrier. You will need to repeat this process a couple of times to make it stick.

Six secrets for having a well-socialized dog:

As mentioned throughout this chapter, the sooner you begin teaching your Morkie proper behavior, the easier it will be. The same applies to teaching your dog to act correctly around other people.

The following six suggestions can be applied to any dog at any age, even an older rescue dog that has issues with strangers. The key is being patient, loving and consistent with your Morkie.

1. Make your pet feel safe and secure: Fear leads to aggression and nervousness. When introducing your Morkie to a new situation or person, make sure your dog feels safe and secure. How can you do that? Let it meet the new person or animal on its own terms; stand close to your dog, so it can hide between your legs if necessary. If meeting a person, ask them to give your Morkie a treat and talk in a low voice.

2. Teach your dog how to play without biting: If you allow your dog to bite you when playing, when it meets a new person or dog, it will assume that biting is an acceptable way of playing. It might accidentally bite a bigger dog and get a bigger bite in return. Or it could bite a small child in the face, leading to your dog needing to be euthanized.

3. Teach your dog to interact with other animals and all types of people: Make sure your Morkie gets to meet as many different people as possible: different races, tall, short, fat, skinny, with beards and canes or umbrellas. The same with animals: introduce it to cats, other dogs, and anything that moves. When it hears new noises, go and investigate together, so it can see that these noises are no threat to it or you.

4. Teach your dog that you are the pack leader: The pack leader protects the family and your puppy will look to you for protection. If it is used to controlling you and making its own decisions, it will assume the responsibility of being your pack leader. So when presented with a stranger or a new situation, it will freak out, bark and act aggressively, because it believes that it needs to protect you.

5. Teach your dog to follow your lead: Your Morkie picks up on your attitude and reactions. When meeting a new person, reach out and shake their hands, if it is an old friend give them a hug, etc. Your dog will observe your behavior and most likely will allow the person to pet it. When meeting dogs, you can pet the dog to show your dog that it is friendly and nice. Do the same with other animals that you and your dog might meet. Your Morkie will follow your lead.

6. Train your dog according to its age: Puppies can't handle more than three to four new tasks a day, and adult dogs maybe four to five new tasks a day. Older dogs or rescued dogs can't handle more than two to three new tasks a day, maybe even less. If your dog doesn't react well to the new situation, but was calm, be sure to praise it, to build up its self-confidence.

Simple reminders for when you are teaching your Morkie socialization skills

The key obedience training and socializing your Morkie is to keep the sessions fun and relaxed. If it is enjoying meeting new people and dogs and learning new obedience commands, it will learn quicker than if it is a chore. If you notice your Morkie is grumpy and not enjoying the training sessions, stop for awhile and do something it really enjoys. Be flexible and make training fun for both of you.

If your Morkie is on the nervous or shy side, you will need to be extra patient and give it the extra time needed. Remember, this isn't a race or competition to teach your Morkie the fastest, you need to teach at a speed that works and allows it to respond to the training. Dogs are like snowflakes; each one is unique. Each dog deserves to be treated uniquely, so work with your own dog's particular needs and personality.

Every year in the United States thousands of dogs are euthanized for bad behavior. Bad behavior can all be avoided by taking the time to teach them when they are young. Even an older dog can be taught good behavior with an extra dose of love. Don't let your Morkie be one the thousands of dogs that are euthanized each year.

Conclusion

"Whoever said you can't buy happiness, forgot little Puppies."

Gene Hill

Your Morkie will give you a lifetime of loyal companionship and joy. Morkies are a crossbreed between a purebred Yorkshire terrier and a Maltese, bringing out the best in already almost-prefect breeds, producing a faithful, intelligent, obedient and playful little Morkie.

Morkies are very intelligent dogs that are eager to please their owners, making them one of the easiest dogs to train. They make an ideal pet for first-time dog owners or elderly ones that lack the mobility for training a dog that is hyperactive and has a hardheaded temperament.

Morkies are appreciated for their easygoing personality and flexible temperament.

Photo Courtesy of
Karen Unger

This book contains everything you need to know about your Morkie. It will help your puppy grow into a happy, well-behaved and obedient dog. The suggestions provided in this book will help you train a puppy or even an older adult Morkie that might have been rescued from an abusive home.

The only thing this book doesn't help you with is to pick out the ideal name for your Morkie. We will leave that difficult task up to you.

The chapter on potty training your Morkie discusses various methods of how to potty train your puppy. If you follow the suggestions given, you should have successfully trained your Morkie in less than a week. If your Morkie is an older adult dog, it will take a little longer than one week and more patience is needed to potty train.

This book also provides practical advice on how to care for your dog's health and how to avoid future illnesses. Also, it goes into detail about how to groom your puppy by yourself and how to brush its teeth.

This book is a handy guide to refer to each time you need to remind yourself of some of the good advice. Keep it in your 'go to' drawer, along with the veterinarian's contact information, grooming receipts and important records.

It is true what the book states about the results of training properly and early. If you follow the guidelines, you are sure to have a wonderful, beautiful addition to your family and your home. You will find that your special friend will add so much joy to your life, guaranteed. Just remember, follow the guidelines and use love and patience.

We wish you and your Morkie a long and happy life together and may this book become your manual to understanding and training your adorable little pet.

Happy Morkie, happy life!

Photo Courtesy of
Ellen Gitlin